The Forgotten Prophet

The Forgotten Prophet

*Bishop Henry McNeal Turner and the
African American Prophetic Tradition*

Andre E. Johnson

LEXINGTON BOOKS
Lanham • Boulder • New York • Toronto • Plymouth, UK

Published by Lexington Books
An imprint of The Rowman & Littlefield Publishing Group, Inc.
4501 Forbes Boulevard, Suite 200, Lanham, Maryland 20706
www.rowman.com

10 Thornbury Road, Plymouth PL6 7PP, United Kingdom

British Library Cataloguing in Publication Information Available

Library of Congress Cataloging-in-Publication Data

The hardback edition of this book was previously cataloged by the Library of Congress as
follows:

Johnson, Andre.
  The forgotten prophet : Bishop Henry Mcneal Turner and the African American
prophetic tradition / Andre Johnson.
  p. cm.
  Includes bibliographical references and index.
  1. Turner, Henry McNeal, 1834-1915. 2. African Methodist Episcopal Church—
History—19th century. 3. African Methodist Episcopal Church—Bishops. 4. Black
theology. 5. African Americans—Religion. 6. Prophecy—Christianity I. Title.
  BX8449.T87 J64 2012
  287/.8092—dc23   2012031393

ISBN 978-0-7391-6714-4 (cloth : alk. paper)
ISBN 978-0-7391-9767-7 (pbk. : alk. paper)
ISBN 978-0-7391-7854-6 (electronic)

Contents

Acknowledgments

I could not have done any of this work alone. In my quest to publish the book, I needed help along the way. First, I would like to thank my doctoral committee— Michael C. Leff, John Angus Campbell, Gray Matthews, and Beverly Bond for guiding me through the dissertation phase of this project and encouraging me to develop the dissertation into a book. I would also like to thank Sandra Sarkela, who sat in on the defense of my dissertation and who served (and still serves) as a mentor to me. She, along with her husband, Pat Mazzeo, encouraged me along the way and they both continue to offer advice and guidance. I also would like to thank the organizers and reviewers of the National Communication Association—especially the African American Communication and Culture and Public Address Divisions for first, allowing me space to present work on Turner and second, for offering critiques that helped sharpen my arguments. I also include in my thanks the National Council of Black Studies for allowing me to present work on Turner as well and Lexington Books for believing and supporting this project.

I would also like to thank Memphis Theological Seminary and another one of my mentors, Barbara A. Holmes, for their unwavering support. I really appreciated the institutional support I received while doing this project. While I would like to thank Steve Edscorn, Jane Williamson, and the fine library staff at Memphis Theological Seminary, I also need to thank Megan Kettner who, when not serving as our technical services librarian, served as my typesetter and proofer. Her contribution has been invaluable in this project. I thank her for her advice and counsel.

I would like to thank my Gifts of Life Ministries family for allowing me to travel, write, and still serve as pastor. I am truly a blessed man of God to serve at G'Life. Finally, I would like to thank my wife Lisa, who has put up with Turner and me for the last five years and now can tell as many Henry McNeal Turner stories as I can.

Acknowledgments

I dedicate this book to my advisor, mentor, colleague and friend, the late Michael C. Leff who, when I attempted to write or say more about Turner than I needed during the dissertation would simply say, "Andre, save it for the book."

Introduction

On January 1, 1866, Henry McNeal Turner was the keynote speaker at the Emancipation Day Celebration in Augusta, Georgia. Organizers billed the day as the "First day of Freedom" and celebrated the ending of the Civil War and the passage of the Thirteenth Amendment that abolished slavery. Many people, both black and white in the audience that day sensed the excitement in the air and were ready to begin the arduous process of building the South through Reconstruction efforts. Turner sensed the mood as well and ended his speech with the charge to blacks in the audience:

> Let us love the whites, and let by-gones be by-gones, neither taunt nor insult them for past grievances, respect them; honor them; work for them; but still let us be men. Let us show them we can be a people, respectable, virtuous, honest, and industrious, and soon their prejudice will melt away, and with God for our father, we will all be brothers. ("Celebration," Jan. 13, 1866)

However, almost thirty years later, Turner's tone changed. With the end of Reconstruction, the 1875 Civil Rights bill declared unconstitutional by the Supreme Court, and the increase in lynching and the gains of Reconstruction disappearing, Turner was no longer optimistic about the future of the United States and the role African Americans would play. In a speech given at the Congress of Africa in Atlanta in 1895, Turner declared, "There is no manhood future in the United States for the Negro" ("American Negro" 194).

This book is an examination the life and career of Bishop Henry McNeal Turner—a study that examines Turner's rhetorical trajectory, from 1866-1895—a trajectory that moves from "let by-gones be by-gones" and "we will be brothers" to "there is no manhood future in the United States for the Negro." It is a story about nineteenth century America and how African Americans found voice and reclaimed agency to speak up and speak out on issues germane to them and their communities. It is also an examination of race and the use of the African American prophetic tradition. It is a story of how Turner's rhetoric shifted over time but stayed primarily rooted within this religious tradition. It is also a story of how someone who would later become a proponent of African emigration as

1

the panacea for African American woes in America, still found relevance as an orator and leader in America.

As an orator, Henry McNeal Turner was one of the finest in America during the Reconstruction and Post-Reconstruction periods. One contemporary said of Turner,

> As an orator, he is one of the most forcible and eloquent in the United States. His sentences weigh more than the ordinary language of most men. When speaking, he is very impressive, and carries an audience with him as easily as the wind sweeps the chaff before it. He has the power of taking hold of his audience and chaining their attention to the subject under consideration. He has been considered by many, one of the best if not the best orator of his class in the United States. (Simmons 818)

Another contemporary called Turner a "Black Moses" (Haley 35), and *Harper's Weekly* noted the success of Turner-led revivals, calling Turner the "Negro Spurgeon" in reference to famed English evangelist Charles Spurgeon (1863). As an evangelist in revivals, observers knew Turner to have mourners "falling around the altar like dead men and women" (Hinton, Oct. 3, 1863). Yet still another observer wrote that no one "spoke more eloquently, more learnedly, more effectively, and enunciated more profoundly the eternal principles of human rights than did Henry McNeal Turner" (Ponton 24).

Early in his public career, he attracted large crowds wherever he went to speak and could command the attention of those crowds when no one else could. Knowing that Turner was in town to speak could get someone to change their plans. A correspondent of the *Christian Recorder* newspaper wrote that when he learned that Turner was to preach in his city, he put on his Sabbath "fixens" and "wended my way thither to hear and be benefited by the solid and unadulterated word expounded by this eminent divine" (Conover, April 4, 1863). Many regarded him as a true champion of the pulpit and some even maintained that while in Washington, Turner was the most influential African American (Hinton, July 4, 1863).

His contemporaries also knew Turner as a great debater. Turner helped institute the Israel Lyceum while pastor there.[1] In one debate Turner, anticipating his progressive thinking with regard to gender during his lifetime, argued the affirmative position on the question, "has not a lady equally a right to court a gentleman, as a gentleman has to court a lady?" After more than three hours of arguments and counterarguments, the judges declared Turner the winner (Hinton, Aug. 8, 1863).

After hearing Turner speak at the Emancipation Day Celebration in Augusta in 1866, Robert Kent wrote about the audience, "Such lofty, eloquent language from a colored man, they had not expected to hear. Even the whites could not conceal their admiration, nor restrain the applause due to him, as the best orator of the day" (Jan. 27, 1866).

Turner's contemporaries admired him for his ability to speak thoroughly on many different subjects—even within one speech. At a Fourth of July celebration, one writer noted that Turner "delivered an able oration, in which he reviewed the History of America from its discovery by Columbus to the present day and was pronounced by white and colored to be the most masterly oration they ever heard" (Saunders, July 21, 1866).

Turner's powerful rhetoric led him to preach integrated revivals, command audiences with Senators, congressional leaders, and presidents, and to become a popular correspondent for the *Christian Recorder* newspaper. His rhetoric helped him become the first African American chaplain in the Armed Forces, an agent for the Freedmen's Bureau, a State Constitutional delegate, and a State Representative. His oratorical powers had a lot to do with him becoming the Presiding Elder of Georgia for his church and eventually Bishop. Along with these accomplishments, Turner was the first African American Postmaster General (Georgia), and offered bills in the Georgia House of Representatives giving all women the right to vote and creating an eight-hour workday.[2] In addition, he was the publication manager (1876-1880) of the African Methodist Episcopal Church (AME), ordained the first women as elder in the AME church—an ordination that the other bishops rescinded, and led hundreds if not thousands of African Americans to Africa. While Marcus Garvey has the distinction of being the leader of the "Back to Africa" movement, Garvey never traveled to African and only "talked" about going to Africa—Turner actually had some success at persuading people to go.

Moreover, while doing all of this, Turner found time to start three newspapers: *Southern Recorder* (1887-1889), *Voice of Missions* (1893-1900) and the *Voice of the People* (1901-1904), serving as editor of all three. He took four trips to Africa himself and established the AME Church there. He also wrote numerous articles and essays for various newspapers, wrote several introductions to books, preached all over the country, and carried out his Episcopal duties. Turner married four times (all of his wives except the last one preceded him in death), and only two of his children—both from his first marriage—survived until adulthood.[3]

In short, Turner lived a very active life and produced a plethora of documents that still survive today. However, history has not been kind to Turner. After Turner's death in 1915, his friend and fellow AME minister Mungo Ponton published an uncritical biographical work on Turner in 1917. After Ponton, it would be 1938 before there was another study on Turner.[4] However, during the 1960s and with the rise of Black Studies departments emphasizing the rediscovery of African American figures, Turner enjoyed minimal attention from scholars in history and religion.[5] After the 1980s, there was some renewal of interest in the life and works of Turner, culminating in Stephen Ward Angell's critical full-length biographical work on Turner, *Bishop Henry McNeal Turner and African American Religion in the South.*[6]

However, while there has been some attention paid to Turner in other disciplines, "Turner scholarship" in the field of rhetoric has been anemic. Despite Turner's massive corpus of speeches, letters, and essays, there have been to date only two dissertations and two published articles that focus on Turner's rhetoric.[7] The reason for this may be found in Turner's rhetoric itself. If people remember Turner at all, it is for his unpopular emigration position. Indeed, Turner's emigration rhetoric took up much of his career. From the time he became a bishop in 1880 until his death, Turner advocated emigration is some form.

However, emigration on the scale Turner advocated did not happen and Turner himself did not emigrate. Therefore, many saw Turner's rhetoric as a failure. Turner was an embarrassment at times within his own church and at other times, especially in his later years, many considered him a laughingstock. Others thought he was just plain "crazy" and many thought Turner's rhetoric was just the ramblings of some "old kook." The more Turner advocated emigration as the panacea for African American problems in America, the further he moved away from mainstream thought in the African American community.

However, as I argue, it would be a mistake to call Turner's rhetoric a failure. Our perceptions of rhetoric must go under alteration before we can understand and appreciate Turner's rhetoric. First, much of Turner's rhetoric was prophetic in nature. Not that Turner predicted impending doom or anything in the future (even though some may argue against this when reading his texts), but Turner, in ancient prophetic tradition, forth told—or spoke truth to power—and called his audiences to live up to the ideals they espoused. In short, through his prophetic pronouncements, announcements, and denouncements, Turner criticized and lambasted not only governmental institutions, but also other African American leaders, his church, and other ministers. No one was exempt from Turner's prophetic wrath.

Second, if we read Turner's rhetoric as prophetic, then we need to invoke another standard of judgment towards his rhetoric. Much rhetorical criticism still focuses on effects or a means to an end. In other words, we judge speaker effectiveness by audience response.[8] If the speaker persuades the audience, it is a good speech—if not, then it is a bad one. Reading Turner through the lens of audience response or effects would render him a failure. Not only would his emigration rhetoric be a failure, but also most of the causes that Turner advocated and supported would be failures.[9]

However, as Robert Terrill noted in his study of Malcolm X, there are other standards of judgment that "suggest other conceptions of rhetoric" (6-8). One of those conceptions is to understand that action does not necessarily have to happen after the speech—that the very rhetoric itself is an action. Here, rhetoric transforms the audience into redefining and reshaping their situations and even themselves. It allows the audience to see themselves in a different light and in so doing, the audience can begin to reclaim agency and create spaces to act and, more importantly, to be. Rhetoric that speaks to the consciousness of the audience—even if the audience rejects the political action that the speaker calls for—still allows the audience to act in the way they see fit.

Not unlike many African Americans during the period in which he lived, Turner faced many rhetorical challenges, and much has been written about the philosophical, political, or social thoughts and traditions that many African Americans grounded themselves in as they strove for economic justice and freedom during this and other time periods of discrimination.[10]

However, many scholars neglect the tradition that arguably is the foundation of other traditions of African American social and political thought—the *religious tradition*. Cornel West writes of this primarily Christian tradition:

> Afro-American thought must take seriously the most influential and enduring intellectual tradition in its experience: evangelical and pietistic Christianity. This tradition began the moment that African slaves, laboring in sweltering heat on plantations owned and ruled primarily by white American Christians, tried to understand their lives and servitude in the light of biblical text, Protestant hymns, and Christian testimonies. . . . This "church," merely a rubric to designate black Christian communities of many denominations, came into being when slaves decided, often at the risk of life and limb, to "make Jesus their choice" and to share with one another their common sense of purpose and Christian understanding of their circumstances. (*Prophesy* 15)

Along with its "priestly streams," this tradition is also the home to a *prophetic stream* of thought. West argues that the "prophetic stream" of thought provided the essence of African American critical thought. Because "every individual regardless of class, country, caste, race, or sex should have the opportunity to fulfill his or her potentialities" (*Prophesy* 16), I argue that this tradition provided the impetus and the critical edge for other African American traditions. Therefore, what I attempt to do in this book is to examine Turner's use of this religious tradition, which manifests itself in Turner's use of prophetic rhetoric.

I need to be clear here. *I am not interested in focusing on whether Turner was a prophet* or *on what makes a prophet a prophet*. What I attempt here is to study Turner's use of *prophetic rhetoric* by examining certain speech texts that function as prophetic discourse. This leads me to examine how Turner adopts a *prophetic persona* in order to produce this oratory along with how Turner shifts his prophetic persona throughout his career to fit the situation in which he finds himself.

I examine these texts by engaging in what rhetoric scholars call *textual criticism* or *close reading*. Defined as an interpretive analysis that primarily examines texts in light of the contexts in which they are given, critics using the textual criticism approach are concerned with the rhetorical dynamics of particular discourses. For textual critics, *theory* arises from an "understanding of the particular;" abstract or theoretical principles are only important within the "texture of an actual discourse" (Leff 378). In short, textual criticism privileges texts and demonstrates how texts functions rhetorically.

McClure argues that, "among the elements involved in textual criticism" (close reading) are "the analysis of the historical and biographical circumstances that generate and form [the text's] composition, the recognition of the basic conceptions that establish the co-ordinates of the text, and an appreciation of the way these conceptions interact within the text and help determine its temporal movement" (426). He further writes:

> Textual criticism (close reading) obligates the critic to commit to analyses that privileged an address as a purposeful discourse that attempts to have a persuasive impact on a specific audience(s) in response to a set of momentary situational concerns with particular attention to the rhetorical properties of the text. In this way, textual criticism (close reading) "retains an audience perspective, but as opposed to neo-Aristotelianism, this perspective does not entail measurement of actual responses." Instead, the critical process seeks to explain how rhetorical performance invites certain kinds of responses. (426)

Thus, a close textual reading allows for the historical and biographical approach of a rhetorical biography as well as a theoretical approach that emphasizes the text and thereby enables the critic to tease out more nuances of the text. In the case of my work, a close textual reading will allow me to focus on Turner's prophetic discourse and to show how that discourse operates within a larger context.

One of the criticisms against using the *close reading* approach is that it slights the context of the speech in favor of a formalist textual reading (Terrill, *Symbolic* 22). Quoting Leff and Sachs, Terrill writes that

> A single-minded concentration on particulars . . . may tend to promote its own kind of formalism—readings that isolate the text and constrain interpretation within the orbit of the text's own construction. (*Symbolic* 22)

Critics using the close reading approach have been sensitive to this charge. Moreover, since Leff challenged rhetorical critics to examine the merits of textual criticism (*Textual Criticism* 1986), many not only have, but by extending the parameters of the enterprise, critics have offered new nuances and approaches to textual criticism, while at the same time addressing previous weaknesses of textual criticism.[11]

Mindful of the potential weaknesses associated with a close reading, I will attempt to present an analysis that examines the text both intrinsically and extrinsically—a reading in and outside the text that will offer a deeper understanding of the times that produced the text as well as the rhetoric used inside the text. Moreover, by using a textual critical approach to analyze Turner's speech texts, I attempt to highlight and acknowledge Turner's own rhetorical agency by examining his prophetic persona.

Prophetic Rhetoric

Prophetic rhetoric does not descend from our traditional, systematized, Greco-Roman model of rhetoric. Prophetic rhetoric comes from the Hebraic tradition found in the writings of the Old Testament in which there is no systematic theory of rhetoric. As Darsey reminds us about the Old Testament prophets, they "left us with a considerable body of discourse, but they were not theorists and were not prone to spend time examining or articulating the assumptions on which their discourse was built" (7).

Another reason for the difficulty of defining prophetic rhetoric may lie in the unwillingness of some to deem credible anything having its foundation in the "Bible, religion, or prophecy." Darsey agrees with this assumption when he states,

> In our everyday usage, we acknowledge the possibility of something like a religious commitment at the base of radical social movements: we talk of revolutionary "faith" and "zeal"; we refer to radical leaders as "prophets"; and we analyze radical rhetoric according to its "God terms" and "devil terms". At the same time, while we admit of the existence of some blatantly "messianic" or "millennial" or "revitalization" movements that have unmistakably religious roots, we are also victims of our own enlightenment and generally prefer explanations of a more secular order. (8)

Therefore, in order to work with "the prophetic," one has to suspend modern tendencies toward rationalized incredulity and "humble ourselves before what we understand only incompletely" (Darsey 8).

Elsewhere, I have defined prophetic rhetoric as *discourse grounded in the sacred and rooted in a community experience that offers a critique of existing communities and traditions by charging and challenging society to live up to the ideals espoused while offering celebration and hope for a brighter future.*[12] Prophetic rhetoric, to use Darsey's words, is "characterized by a steadfast refusal to adapt itself to the perspectives of its audience, a rhetoric in extremis, indicating something more complex than the breakdown of order; it indicates an alternative order" (5-6). Prophetic rhetoric dedicates itself to the rights of individuals, especially the poor, marginalized, and exploited members of society. It intends to lift the people to an ethical conception of the Deity (Heschel 413).

Prophetic rhetoric then acts also as social criticism because it "challenges the leaders, the conventions, the ritual practices of a particular society" by way of what society deems sacred (Walzer 33). Prophetic rhetoric also becomes a critical rhetoric that "examines the dimensions of domination and freedom as these are exercised in relativized world" (McKerrow 91).

This definition explicates a four-part rhetorical structure. *First, speakers must ground prophetic discourse in what the speaker and the audience deem as sacred.* In short, the speaker must appeal to something that both speaker and audience hold as sacred. For a *prophet* to ground herself in anything *sacred* that the audience does not recognize as such would render that message unimportant.

This means that the prophet is indeed part of the community fabric and understands the beliefs of the audience. Therefore, there is no prophetic discourse outside of community. In studying the prophets of the Bible, Paul Hanson argues that the "prophets spoke out of a distinct tradition, drew upon a carefully developed worldview and defended a social system characterized by well-defined values and warrants" (3). Moreover, for Hanson, prophets were not "solitary individualists acting out of private and inscrutable impulse" (3), they were people rooted in community and who participated in community traditions and beliefs.

Therefore, prophetic rhetoric highlights this communal identity by lifting up and reminding the people of whatever is sacred. Darsey writes that "Walter Brueggemann describes the prophet as one who must "move back into the deepest memories of his community and activate those very symbols that have always been the basis for contradicting the regent consciousness" (20).

Second, there is an element of consciousness-raising through a sharing or an announcement of the real situation. In prophetic rhetoric, the prophet speaks the *already known and bears witness to what the speaker believes as the truth.* Therefore, instead of an unveiling, it becomes more of a revealing. By this revealing, the prophet goes beneath the surface and states the obvious that others might be afraid to speak. It is consciousness-raising because once it is out in the open, the prophetic desire is that the audience reflects on the situation with the hope of changing its ways.

This is reminiscent of the children's story *The Emperor's New Clothes.* Everyone knows that the Emperor is naked but yet is afraid to say anything. It is only when a child states the obvious that everybody finally acknowledges the fact that the Emperor is indeed naked. Once this fact becomes a shared reality, it is the speaker's hope that the "people" can start addressing the problem.

This element of prophetic rhetoric is also very similar to the classical rhetorical term *parrhesia.* Defined as *frank or boldness of speech,* parrhesia involved the critical telling of the truth within uncomfortable situations because a speaker felt it was her duty to speak (Foucault 9-23). However, the difference between parrhesia and *prophetic parrhesia* consists in the sacred grounding of the prophetic speech.

The third element in the rhetorical structure is the charge, challenge, critique, judgment, or warning of the audience(s). While still being grounded in the sacred and communal values traditions, and beliefs of the audience, the speaker/prophet then charges, challenges, critiques, or renders judgment or warnings not only to the assembled audience, but also toward much wider audiences, or to institutions and society in general. The speaker usually does this by offering reinterpretations of what is sacred and begins to cast a vision of the world not as it is, but as it could and should be.

The final part of the prophetic rhetorical structure is the offer of encouragement and hope. The prophet/speaker has been grim about the prospects of what she is championing, but typically ends her speech in a hopeful or encouraging declaration.

In prophetic rhetoric, there are two types of hope. The first is an *eschatological hope*. It is a hope mainly in the afterlife. This hope is usually associated with apocalyptic prophecy. However, the second type of hope is a pragmatic hope. The hope is more of an earthly hope—more of a pragmatic hope that is rooted in the prophet's faith in God. Cornel West calls this hope a "tragicomic hope." About this experience West writes,

> Tragicomic hope is rooted in a love of freedom. It proceeds from a free inquisitive spirit that highlights imperial America's weak will to racial justice. It is a sad yet sweet indictment of abusive power and blind greed run amok. It is a melancholic yet melioristic stance toward America's denial of its terrors and horrors heaped on others. It yields a courage to hope for betterment against the odds without a sense of revenge or resentment. It revels in a dark joy of freely thinking, acting, and loving under severe constraints of unfreedom. (West, *Democracy* 216)

Types of Prophetic Rhetoric

Traditionally, critics studying prophetic rhetoric locate the genre within two primary traditions. The first is apocalyptic prophecy. Brummett offers a working definition of apocalyptic rhetoric by calling it a "mode of thought and discourse that empowers its audience to live in a time of disorientation and disorder by revealing to them a fundamental plan within the cosmos." Further, he writes that apocalyptic rhetoric is "discourse that restores order through structures of time and history by revealing the present to be a pivotal moment in time" (9). In addition, apocalyptic rhetoric acts as an unveiling and a revealing that assumes a position of having knowledge through visions, dreams, or meditations that the prophet/speaker shares with the audience. It is a secret or divine revelation revealed only to the prophet and it becomes the speaker's job to disclose the previously hidden.

Ronald Reid argues that apocalyptic discourse has a three part rhetorical structure. First, the vision explains the distressing present, and the distressing present is part of "God's plan of history." Second, the vision provides reassurance for the future and finally, in apocalyptic discourse, the speaker assures the audience that the end is at hand and that they must remain faithful while God is at work (237-238). In short, what apocalyptic rhetoric promises is the "inevitable and cataclysmic end of the oppressor" through some major move of God (*Malcolm X* 28).

However, the more popular of the two is the Jeremiad. The term jeremiad, meaning a lamentation or doleful compliant, derives from the Old Testament prophet Jeremiah, who warned of Israel's fall and the destruction of Jerusalem. The fall came because of the people's failure to keep the Mosaic covenant. However, even though Jeremiah denounces Israel's wickedness and prophesies-

destruction in the short term, he always looks for the day when the nation would repent and be restored (Howard-Pitney 6).

Like apocalyptic prophecy, the jeremiad has a three-part rhetorical structure. First, the speaker cites the promise. Second, there is criticism of the present declension or retrogression from the promise, and finally there is a resolving prophecy that society will shortly complete its mission and redeem the promise (Howard-Pitney 7). In other words, the speaker reminds the people of the promise; usually some sacred promise that they are "chosen." Then the speaker criticizes the people for failing to live up to the promise, and finally the speaker calls the people back to the promise or the "covenant." Failure to come back and to live up to the covenant will bring even harsher judgment (usually from God) on the people. Therefore, the speaker acts as social critic reminding the people of who they are.

African American Prophetic Tradition

African American speakers have used these two types of prophetic discourses in powerful ways. One only has to look at David Walker's *Appeal* for a good example of apocalyptic discourse and Martin Luther King's *I Have a Dream* speech for an example of the jeremiad. Indeed, much scholarship examines how African Americans used and appropriated these two subgenres of prophetic rhetoric to appeal to their audiences.

However, what happens when a speaker cannot use or appropriate an apocalyptic or jeremiadic appeal? What if the speaker does not believe that God will cause a cataclysmic event that will bring in a new age? What if a speaker does not appeal to a covenant—or for that matter, does not believe the covenant is available to the people? What if the covenant itself is the problem—can one still engage in prophetic discourse? I suggest that one can engage in prophetic discourse simply because not all prophetic discourse fits the apocalyptic and jeremiad types. In short, what I attempt to demonstrate in this volume is that, especially in the African American rhetorical tradition, speakers had to develop other forms of prophetic discourse in order to appeal to and move their audiences.

Drawing from the career of Henry McNeal Turner, I note four other types of prophetic rhetoric. The first is *celebratory prophecy*. I define celebratory prophecy as a prophecy, typically grounded in a sacred covenant that calls the people to celebrate an event that leads the people to celebrate the sacred (covenant). In other words, before the event, the prophet could not invoke the covenant because the audience that the prophet represents was not included in the covenant. Moreover, the prophet links the event to the will of God, thus becoming a sacred event worthy of celebration.

Like the others, this type of prophecy has a three-part rhetorical structure. First, the prophet announces the reason for celebration. Second, the prophet chronicles reasons why celebration was not available in the past. This usually involves the second part of rhetorical discourse—sharing of the real situation by engaging in a recall of event. Here the prophet engages in constructing a sacred history that allows the audience to remember the past. However, the prophet does not intend for the people to become bitter and angry about the past, but to become empowered by seeing how God intervened in history. Here the prophet resembles the biblical prophet Moses. For example, when Moses asks the people to remember, it is not so that they can become angry with their oppressors, but so they can see the work of God within their history. Finally, the prophet calls the people to see a new era, a new relationship, as a new people.

What I am calling celebratory prophecy is similar to Jones and Rowland's *covenant affirming jeremiad*. The covenant affirming jeremiad differs from the traditional jeremiad in that instead of rebuking the audience because it has fallen away from the covenant and needs to return, this version of the genre celebrates the fact that the covenant has not been abridged; therefore, a return is not needed. Jones and Rowland explain:

> Rather than argue that the nation had violated its basic covenant, [the speaker] affirms the values behind an essentially mythic view of the meaning of the nation. . . . In this essentially optimistic vision, a commitment to basic values [points] the way to ideological adaptation that in turn would lead to the stronger nation that was predicted in the mythic vision in which the values were grounded. (161)

Therefore, the covenant affirming jeremiad is a "rhetorical form in which an optimistically grounded narrative is used to affirm basic values" (Jones and Rowland 162). Moreover, the mythic narrative solves any problem, issues, or concern the people face. Thus, as Jones and Rowland argue, "the warning is not that the covenant has been broken, but a positive call for ideological adaptation in order to guarantee that the mythic vision of a better nation is achieved" (162). By combining elements of the traditional jeremiad (the warnings, problems, and concerns) with the belief that the covenant has not been broken, the covenant affirming jeremiad can unify as well as give warning of what Jones and Rowland call "ideological calcification" (160).

As I will demonstrate in chapter 1, a close reading of Turner's *Emancipation Day* speech reveals that Turner's rhetoric fits better under *celebratory prophecy*. I believe that it cannot be considered apocalyptic because he does not foretell impending doom—nor could it be considered a typical jeremiad because the people have not strayed away from the covenant, and they are not warned of dire consequences if they do not live up to those ideals.

While Turner does not argue that the nation has "violated its basic covenant" and while he definitely affirms the "values behind this mythic view," Turner's speech is not a covenant affirming jeremiad. First, the speech is not a jeremiad in the traditional definition or in the covenant affirming version because Turner offers no warnings at all. There is no call for an ideological adaptation to anything because the people have already adapted by eradicating slavery and passing the Thirteenth Amendment, which calls for a celebration for all people.

Moreover, what the covenant affirming jeremiad assumes is that the people should celebrate the covenant. However, what celebratory prophecy does is to celebrate the *event* so that the *covenant* may be worthy of celebration. Again, as I will demonstrate in chapter 1, by mentioning the horrors of slavery and the Civil War, Turner reminds his audience prophetically that America has not always lived up to the covenant and because of that, blacks really had no reason to celebrate the covenant. However, because of recent events, blacks are free and, for Turner at least, blacks are now citizens who can enjoy celebrating the mythic view of America. Therefore, unlike the covenant affirming jeremiad, which celebrates the covenant unconditionally, celebratory prophecy celebrates *the event, which leads to a celebration of the covenant*. In other words, America is the land of liberty because for Turner, America has now demonstrated this belief by its actions; therefore, there is reason to celebrate.

The second type of prophecy used by African Americans is a *prophetic disputation* or *disputation prophecy*. From his study of the biblical prophets of the Old Testament, Adrian Graffy writes that disputation occurs when the speaker offers a "quotation of the people's opinion" within the speech context and offers a refutation "which corrects this opinion" (105). He explicitly notes the speaker's "quotation of the people's opinion" and refutation of that opinion as the important distinguishing factors in naming a speech a disputation because previous studies on disputation have included texts where the speaker may only *imply the people's opinion,* and texts where a refutation of the implied opinion is not offered (2-23).

There is a three-part rhetorical structure to the prophetic disputation. First, the prophet must establish her or his position on the issue the people are debating. This must be a clear-cut and strong position, and the people cannot see the prophet waiver on this position. Second, the prophet must dispute and refute the claims of her or his opponents. Finally, the prophet gives warnings or announces judgments that will happen if the people do not adhere to the prophecies the prophet declares. Thus, drawing from Graffy's basic definition of disputation, in chapter 2 I maintain that Turner's *Eligibility* speech belongs to a type of deliberative oratory that is also a *prophetic disputation*.

When Turner stood and spoke that day on the floor of the House, he had heard the arguments of his opponents, incorporated many of those same arguments in his speech to dispute and refute. "What is it that the Negro race has done," "the Negro is charged with holding office," "it is said that Congress never gave us the right to hold office," and "we are told we have no right to hold office," are all arguments or, in the words of Graffy, "opinions of the people," that Turner refuted.

The prophetic disputation functions much like Gregg's *ego-function of protest rhetoric*. Recalling that prophetic rhetoric sometimes acts as protest rhetoric, Gregg argues that protest rhetoric is rhetoric that "appeals to the protestors

themselves who feel the need for psychological refurbishing and affirmation."
Gregg further writes:

> Spokesmen for protest movements also become surrogates for others who share
> their intimate feelings of inadequacy. The rhetoric is basically self-directed, not
> other-directed in the usual sense of that term, and thus it can be said to be ful-
> filling an ego-function. (74)

Gregg defines what he means by the ego-function of rhetoric. For Gregg the
ego-function is two-fold—first it is the "act of communication wherein one's
self is the primary audience and where others identify with the rhetoric insofar
as they share similar ego-concerns," and second, the ego-function of rhetoric
constitutes "self-hood through expression that is establishing, defining, and affirming one's self-hood as one engages in a rhetorical act" (74).

Prophetic disputations function rhetorically primarily because they give the
speaker a chance not only to speak about the evils perpetrated by his opponents,
but also to do so in a way that creates a sense of empowerment, not only for the
speaker but also for the community the speaker represents. In this way, prophetic disputations are similar to Gregg's ego-function of protest rhetoric because the prophet aims the rhetoric at the "protestors themselves," the ones who
are in need of affirmation of their personhood. While Turner aims his rhetoric
towards his opponents, the main thrust of his message appeals to his supporters—the ones *who felt like Turner* but somehow did not have the skill, acumen,
or courage to *speak like Turner*.

However, prophetic disputations and, for that matter, prophetic rhetoric in
general, do not follow Gregg's view that the speaker needs *self-affirmation* and
that the speaker is the *primary audience* of the message. What Gregg assumes is
that the speaker also needs this psychological refurbishing and affirmation—and
maybe in protest rhetoric, the speaker does. However, with prophetic rhetoric,
the speaker needs no such affirmation. With prophetic rhetoric, before the
speaker speaks, affirmation comes from God. In other words, the speaker does
not need approval or affirmation from anyone to speak. The speaker's ego is in
check because the ego, the self, in fact the whole person of the speaker, belongs
to God.

The third type of prophecy used by African Americans is what I call *mission-oriented prophecy*. I define a mission-oriented prophecy as a constitutive
rhetoric that calls a people to participate in a divine mission by reconstituting the
people from their perceived identities. While a constitutive rhetoric assumes that
audiences are already a rhetorical effect and uses that identify to shape the message, a mission-oriented prophecy finds the constructed identities problematic
and offers a new vision or identity for the people. Therefore, what the prophet
does is to (re)constitute the people in an identity that would fit the divine call.

In chapter 3, I argue that in his *Negro Convention* speech, Turner engaged
in mission-oriented prophecy. Drawing on historical as well as contemporary
situations affecting the plight of African Americans, Turner's goal was to bring

forth a people that would take charge of their current situation. Turner's goal was to get his audience to participate in the narratives in which he was casting.

What Turner did in the narrative was to demonstrate the loyalty and faithfulness of African Americans while he challenged them to be just as faithful and loyal to *themselves* as they have been to a country that did not care anything about them. His goal was to get his audience to see that America was never going to grant citizenship rights to African Americans and that the people needed a mass emigration movement. By showing them that they identified more to their foreparents than the Founding Fathers or "traditional Americanism," Turner hoped that he could call a group of people into being to forge a new destiny, grounded in the belief that God has called this particular group of people to act within a divine mission.

There is a three-part rhetorical structure associated with mission-oriented prophecy. First, the prophet typically attacks the premise of the people's identity. This leads to the second part: the prophet invites the audience to see and participate in the new identity. Third, the prophet offers reasons for the change, and finally, the prophet offers the call to participate in the divine mission as a new people.

The fourth type of prophecy use by African Americans is a type of prophetic discourse which I call *pessimistic prophecy* or the *prophetic lament*. While on the surface a pessimistic prophecy is in contradiction to my earlier definition of prophetic rhetoric's hope and encouragement, the pessimistic prophecy is both pessimistic and hopeful at the same time. For many black orators, finding the racism too entrenched and the American covenant ideals not realistic for black Americans to ascertain, they become wailing and moaning prophets within what I call the *lament tradition* of prophecy. In this tradition, the prophet's primary function is to speak out on the behalf of others and to chronicle their pain and suffering as well as her or his own. By speaking, the prophet offers hope and encouragement to others by acknowledging their sufferings and letting them know that they are not alone.

Traditionally a lament is a woeful complaint done primarily in private by an individual that highlights issues and problems that a person or group faces. Usually this compliant is directly addressed to God in prayer and loaded with rhetorical questions of "why." "Why am I going through this?" "Why am I still feeling all alone?" and "Why is this happening to me?" are standard laments when individuals are feeling the burden of explaining the unexplainable.

Laments are expressions of grief and pain that are in search of an outlet. The one practicing lamentation understands that nothing will change about her or his situation (at least not immediately), but the chance to express oneself and to really speak one's mind becomes therapeutic for the person and abates, at least for a while, the frustration the person feels about the situation. Lamentation then helps a person continue with the struggle, and while not understanding the why questions, the person is still able to function and maintain, thankful that at least God hears her or his cry.

While lamentations are many times private, they can become public through a prophetic declaration. When the prophet does this, she invites all who hear (or read) her words to understand the frustration and pain that the community shares and, consistent with the lament tradition, the prophet does not expect anything to immediately change. The goal here is simply *to speak and to get the audience to hear,* thus becoming a record chronicling the pains and sufferings of the people the prophet claims to represent and to give voice to the voiceless.

In speaking of black prophetic practices, Cornel West argued, "at some point the odds seem so overwhelming, the incorporative strategies of the status quo so effective and the racism so deeply entrenched in American life that a pessimistic attitude can easily develop." However, this is not a defeatist position because as West noted, "Most prophetic practices among black Americans have given this pessimism *an aggressiveness* such that it becomes sobering rather than disenabling, a stumbling block rather than a dead end, a challenge to meet rather than a conclusion to accept" (93).

West grounds his theory of aggressive pessimism in the belief that "black prophetic Americans" eventually become frustrated "regarding the possibilities of fundamental transformation of American society and culture" (93). Therefore, black prophetic Americans, sensing the blatant racism within the American terrain, begin to call into question or challenge the very idea of the covenant as well as the overall fabric of American society.

McLaren and Dantley write that aggressive pessimism has a way of "awakening a new zeal" and that it "restores for African Americans the courage to renew their struggle to appropriate the hegemonic traditions and to resist those societal forms that simply do not make sense to them, namely those that exclude them, that predict and label them, and that sonorously silence them" (39-40). In short, aggressive pessimism helps speakers deal with those insurmountable obstacles placed in front of them, thereby becoming a coping strategy, which starves off communal nihilism and self-destruction (Dantley 274-275).

In chapter 4, I argue that Turner, in his *Fatherland* address, engages in a pessimistic prophecy. For the last twenty years of his life, Turner's primary focus was to chronicle the sufferings of poor African Americans who he felt that mainstream society as well as many "well to do" African Americans had forgotten. He rejected the covenantal rhetoric because he did not believe African Americans would ever be a part, and while he believed that God would eventually judge America for its indifference towards blacks, that judgment was not coming soon. Therefore, within the lament tradition of prophecy, Turner found a space to voice his pessimistic prophecy.

There is a three-part rhetorical structure with this type of discourse as well. First, the speaker often recalls past events to lay claim on the present conditions of the people the prophet represents. Second, within this framework, the speaker then chronicles the sufferings of the people, offering the prophetic lament. Finally, the prophet encourages the people that while nothing will change in the present, the people are not alone—the prophet hears and will represent the voice of the voiceless and reminding others that not all is well.

Prophetic Persona

As I have mentioned earlier, I am not interested in arguing whether or not Turner was a prophet. My argument is that he adopted a rhetorical strategy of *persona* in order to get his messages heard. Since at its foundational level rhetoric is discourse intentionally organized in a message that is goal oriented, personas are rhetorical strategies that allow speakers to "don an assumed character in order to build authority and invoke cultural traditions of their audience" (Lawrence 36). One persona available to speakers is that of prophet. As I argue elsewhere, one reason why speakers would adopt a persona is to dictate the rhetorical situation. Drawing from Lloyd Bitzer, the rhetorical situation is

> a natural context of persons, events, objects, relations, and an exigency which strongly invites utterance; this invited utterance participants naturally in the situation, is in many instances necessary to the completion of situational activity, and by means of its participation with situation obtains its meaning and its rhetorical character. (219)

In short, Bitzer argues that the rhetorical situation creates rhetoric for the appropriate and fitting response.

However, the major problem with the rhetorical situation is that it is an arbitrary construction, as others have argued. It does not take into consideration what the rhetor does to (re)create the rhetorical situation. In short, how does the rhetor discern the *sign of the times*, and begin to speak into that situation? This is especially important to remember when understanding prophetic persona. It is important because in the case of prophetic rhetoric, humans do not select the situation, God does. Therefore, it becomes the duty of the prophet to discern the context that (re)creates the rhetorical situation, which then leads the speaker to say the fitting and appropriate response. In other words, especially for prophetic discourse, the discerned context helps shape the discourse.

However, while there have been studies on personas and even prophetic personas, there have not been studies on the types of prophetic personas. Moreover, speakers adopt prophetic personas depending on the situation or context. In the case of Turner, I argue that he develops at least four types of personas throughout his career.

The first type of persona is a *universal/covenantal prophetic persona*. I define this type of prophetic persona as one in which the prophet sees herself as prophet to all the people and grounded in the sacred covenant of the people. In his *Emancipation Day* (chapter 2) speech, Turner sees himself as the one who knew the mind and will of God for the situation in which Southerners found themselves. Turner calls on both blacks and whites to "let bygones be bygones" and issues a challenge for both races to work together to make America the country it could become. This could happen now because of Emancipation and because society opened the sacred covenant of America to African Americans.

As people began to challenge the gains of Emancipation, Turner shifted from a universal/covenant prophet to a *representative prophet*. I define this persona as one in which the prophet represents the issues of a particular group. No longer tied to the covenantal promises (because usually they have been taken away), the prophet nevertheless becomes the spokesperson for a group of people who typically have no one to speak up for them. In his *Eligibility* speech, Turner represents the interest of African Americans.

The third type of prophetic persona is to become what I call a pragmatic prophet. I define this type of persona as one in which the prophet searches for partners in the prophetic enterprise. Contrary to popular beliefs, prophets are not loners who come from the mountain with a word from on high, but ones who listen for the voice of God in all places and spaces. This could lead many to see the prophet as capitulating to the authorities or giving in to declared enemies. However, for the prophet, it is an opportunity for the people to see some gains from a prophetic endeavor.

The fourth type of prophetic persona is to become what I call a *pessimistic prophet*. I define this type of persona as one in which the prophet, through the lament tradition of prophecy, chronicles the pain and sufferings of the people the prophet represents. This pessimism usually comes at a time when others see the situation as hopeful and pronounce brighter days ahead.

Henry McNeal Turner

Turner was born a "free black" in New Berry Courthouse, South Carolina on February 1, 1834.[13] His father died when he was quite young. His mother Sarah, and maternal grandmother Hannah Greer raised him, and even though he was born a free person, he nonetheless experienced the harsh realities of prejudice and racism. He worked alongside enslaved Africans from sun-up to sundown for meager earnings in South Carolina cotton fields. In winter months, he labored in a blacksmith shop, watched over by harsh, white overseers. This early exposure to the "real world" made him physically strong, and painfully aware of society's inhumane treatment of black people.

Like many great figures in the Old Testament of the Bible, dreams played an important role in Turner's life. When Turner was "eight or nine years old," he had a dream that was both prophetic and propelling. In the dream, he was in front of a large crowd of both blacks and whites, who were looking to him for instruction (Culp 42). He interpreted the dream as God "marking him" for great things. This became a "guiding star" in Turner's life—a point that he would always reflect on when times got tough (Angell, *Bishop* 9).

It also gave him a passion for education. This was no easy task, however, as state laws forbade blacks to attend school or learn to read and write. After managing to obtain a spelling book, Turner attempted to learn how to read and write with the help of people in his community. However, each time he would begin to study, others would find out and have the teaching stopped. Turner, therefore, decided to teach himself,[14] through the help of a divine "dream angel" that Turner believed appeared to him in his dreams to help him learn. Reflecting on this time, he shared with author William Simmons on his dream angel escapade:

> I would study with all the intensity of my soul until overcome by sleep at night; then I would kneel down and pray, and ask the Lord to teach me what I was not able to understand myself, and as soon as I would fall asleep an angelic personage would appear with open book in hand and teach me how to pronounce every word that I failed in pronouncing while awake, and on each subsequent day the lessons given me in my dreams would be better understood than any other portions of the lessons. This angelic teacher, or dream teacher, at all events, carried me through the old Websters spelling book and thus enabled me to read the Bible and hymnbook. (Simmons 807)

From this, Turner not only taught himself how to read and write, but by the time he was fifteen he had read the entire Bible five times and memorized lengthy passages of scripture, which helped him develop a very strong memory (Simmons 807; Batten 233).

After his mother married Jabez Story, the family moved to Abbeville, South Carolina, where Turner found employment as a janitor in a law office. The lawyers were impressed with his "astonishing memory, honed by memorizing passages of scripture" (Angell, *Bishop* 20). They took notice of his "quick mind" and his "eagerness to learn," and furthered Turner's education by teaching him "arithmetic, astronomy, geography, history, law and even theology," which he greatly appreciated. Reflecting on this, he saw it as the answer to his prayers (Angell, *Bishop* 10).

In 1848, Turner attended revival services with his mother and joined the Southern Methodist Church. However, his conversion actually came three years later in 1851, under the preaching of plantation missionary Samuel Leard. Soon after his conversion, Turner accepted the call to preach.

The Southern Methodist Episcopal Church licensed Turner to preach at the age of nineteen. Three years later, at the age of 22, Turner married 19-year-old Eliza Ann Peacher of Columbia, South Carolina. Peacher's father was a carpenter and believed to be the "wealthiest colored man in Columbia" at the time of their marriage. Henry and Eliza would have several children, but only two, John and David, reached adulthood.

Eliza provided much-needed support during this time in Turner's career. While, as Angell notes, information about Turner's career during these years is incomplete, we do know that he was highly successful in his preaching (Angell, *Bishop* 23). One of the first places he preached was Macon, Georgia, where he received a warm welcome from both black and white audiences. It was here that his education from the lawyers in Abbeville served him well. Turner surprised many in the audience with the amount of knowledge he displayed. Benjamin Tanner, who later became an opponent to Turner's emigration plans wrote, "that when they heard him quote history, ecclesiastical and profane, some of the white people declared him to be *a white man galvanized*" (416, emphasis in original).

However, some in Macon believed Turner just memorized sermons and could not speak impromptu. A man by the name of Robert Smith issued Turner a challenge to expound from a text that Smith would give. Turner accepted the challenge and, "in the Spirit of the Lord," he expounded on Genesis 7:1, "Come thou and all thy house into the ark" (Anderson 24-25). While we do not know exactly what Turner said, Anderson reports that not only were the "white citizens well pleased with it," but after the sermon, an offering was called for and $810 was raised (25), a small fortune in that day.

Turner was also instrumental at conducting a series of revivals in Athens, Georgia during the spring of 1858. Paired with W.A. Parks, a white minister who held the post of "missionary" to blacks, Turner preached "powerful sermons" and held the pulpit of the black Methodist church "up to twice a day during the week" (Angell, *Bishop* 29).

Turner traveled to St. Louis where he officially joined the African Methodist Episcopal Church (AME). He had become disillusioned with the Southern Methodist Church because they did not allow blacks to become ordained or to become bishops. He had learned about the AME Church during a visit to New Orleans for a preaching assignment where he also met Willis H. Revels, pastor of the St. James AME Church. Revels shared the story of church's beginnings, along with describing its founder and first bishop, Richard Allen. Turner was thoroughly impressed, as he had not heard of this denomination before and the fact that this was a black Methodist denomination, complete with black bishops and pastors, only intrigued Turner more. However, while documents show that Turner later wrote that he joined the church immediately after Revels invitation, he kept his standing as a licensed minister for the Southern Methodist Church for almost a year after meeting with Revels. He did not join the AME Church until August 1858 (Angell, *Bishop* 29-32).

While Turner had enjoyed some success as a Southern Methodist preacher, it was after he joined the AME Church that his preaching career really took off. After joining the AME Church, Turner moved to Baltimore to serve as pastor of Waters' Chapel AME Church and the Tissue Street Mission. Turner took advantage of more educational opportunities by studying grammar, Latin, Greek, theology, and the classics over the next four years (Simmons 810). Ponton later described the true depths of Turner's desire for an education:

> In procuring his education he was a most painstaking man. Whatever subject he undertook to study . . . he went to the heart of it. He understood thoroughly what many of the school men but half understood . . . he would go a thousand miles to hear a man speak, or to get a new idea on an important subject. [He] sought words from every possible source to express his meaning. (123)

After leaving Baltimore in 1862, Turner served as pastor of the large and influential Israel AME Church in Washington, D.C. Here Turner formed relationships that would serve him throughout his life. He befriended "powerful Republican politicians" such as Thaddeus Stevens, Salmon Chase, Benjamin Wade, and Charles Sumner. Since Turner's church was within walking distance from the Capitol, Turner invited his newfound friends to speak to the black citizens of the city, and he spent hours in the Capitol listening to debates and arguments on the floor of the House of Representatives and the Senate Chamber. Turner quickly learned about the Constitution, the Declaration of Independence, about politics, and the art of deliberative oratory. During this time, Turner also started a lyceum at Israel Church, in which he served as president and participated in debates about these and many other issues of the day (Angell, *Bishop* 36-37). As an AME minister, not only was Turner ordained, but he also became a regular correspondent for the *Christian Recorder*, the AME's weekly newspaper.

During the Civil War, President Abraham Lincoln commissioned Turner to the office of Chaplain in the Union Army, making him the first black chaplain in any branch of the military. In this capacity, he also became a war correspondent and published many articles in the *Christian Recorder* about the trials and tribulations of the First Regiment of U.S. Colored Troops. When the Civil War ended, The Freedmen's Bureau assigned him to Georgia as Army Chaplain.

After his service in the military, Turner turned his attention to politics. During the period of Reconstruction, and while working with the Freedmen's Bureau, Turner became a Republican Party organizer and helped recruit and organize black voters throughout Georgia. He helped establish the first Republican State Convention, assisted in drafting a new state constitution, and served as a Georgia State Representative. However, his victory was short-lived because white members of the state legislature voted to disqualify blacks from holding elected office.

After his ouster from the Georgia state legislature, Turner became United States Postmaster in Macon, Georgia, the first black ever to hold that position. However, pressures began to mount on the federal government to dismiss Turner based on trumped up improprieties. Fired after only two weeks in office, Turner then took a position as a customs inspector in Savannah, Georgia. He held this position for several years, but eventually resigned from this position because of increasing demands of the church (Simmons 816).

After resigning from his position as customs inspector, Turner focused his efforts on building the AME Church in the South. His primary goal was to increase membership and build churches. By 1876, his hard work paid off and he became publications manager for the AME Church. This allowed him to travel to all the districts and meet pastors and leaders of local churches. During the four years he served as publications manager, he developed a following that led to his election as one of the twelve bishops of the church. As a bishop, Turner had a national platform to espouse his ideas on race, politics, lynching, and other social issues of the day, especially emigration.

In the latter part of the nineteenth century, after several failed attempts at an emigration plan, and with the rise of Booker T. Washington and W.E.B. DuBois as leaders in the black community, Turner's influence began to wane. Undaunted, Turner remained active. He served as chair of the board of Morris Brown College from 1896-1908, and kept a busy schedule up to the end of his life. He was in Windsor, Ontario, at the General Conference of the AME Church in 1915 when he suffered a massive stroke. He died hours later at a Windsor hospital (Angell, *Bishop* 248).

The Rhetorical Education of Henry McNeal Turner

Shirley Wilson Logan defines rhetorical education as the "various combinations of experiences influencing how people understand and practice effective communication" (3). Further, she suggests that rhetorical education "occurs at the intersection of symbol use and symbol reception" and that "sites of rhetorical education—defined as involving the act of communicating or receiving information through writing, speaking, reading or listening—are located in those spaces where people and language and a need to communicate come together" (3-4). This site then becomes a place for rhetorical education when learning about rhetoric occurs. While African Americans in the nineteenth century typically were not formally trained in rhetoric, Logan argues that the "application of theoretical principles occurred nonetheless" in these sites of rhetorical education (3).

Turner's rhetorical education starts at the feet of his grandmother Hannah. Turner's grandmother shared stories with the family, and one of those stories was about Turner's grandfather, David Greer. The story went that Greer, captured as a slave and brought to America, had to be released because of a British law that forbade the "enslavement of royal blood" (Angell 7). While the authenticity of this story is a matter of debate, Turner believed it and it became the impetus for his fascination with Africa and all that it represented.

It was stories such as these, and others the elders shared, which influenced Turner and probably taught him the value and power of *storytelling*—a skill Turner found valuable throughout his public speaking career. Ponton noted that Turner was a "good storyteller" and could "call up" stories whenever the occasion fit.

> This power . . . made him an interesting talker and also enabled him . . . to rehearse many of those old fireside tales with a weirdness, almost akin to reality. He told these stories as they were told by his suffering people, under the dim glare of a flickering light, when he was a lad: and it was these stories and tales of suffering, or torture and hardships that helped to make him the great champion for human rights he became in after-years—for they fired his heart and stirred his soul. (Ponton 6-8)

It is interesting to note that Ponton used the word *power* to denote Turner's storytelling abilities. In sharing her teachings with her grandson, Hannah Greer drew from the deep well of African oral traditions, of which storytelling was an integral part. In fact, many Africans believed that there was "power" in the spoken word as many African creation stories attest.

Lampe echoes Ponton's assessment of the African storyteller:

> [Africans] considered sound to be of importance and they produced an oral tradition aimed at keeping the ears rather than the eyes sharpened. . . . Storytellers artfully combined narratives with song, striking, imagery, and metaphors, and an exhilarating oral style to bring a folk tale to light. While telling a tale, the storyteller produced sounds and noises to enhance the story. He chanted, mimicked, rhymed, and used his body to create sound and to suggest different characters (3-4).

While Turner learned much that would help him as an orator by listening to his grandmother and other elders in the community share stories, he also benefited from the spirituals sung by enslaved people. As with storytelling, singing was an integral part of the African traditions that Africans maintained when forced into slavery. These songs were not just for entertainment, they "served to preserve communal values and solidarity," along with providing "refreshment and renewal amid the usual drudgery of slave life" (Lampe 5).

Enslaved people filled the spirituals with a heavy use of "metaphor, innuendo, and indirection," and Lampe noted that the reason for this was that the enslaved people wanted to "express themselves to one another in the presence of whites." Writing about Frederick Douglass' experience as one of the enslaved listening to songs, Lampe wrote, "The slaveholder may have heard in the songs unmeaning jargon, but for slaves the songs were full of meaning" (5). Part of that meaning for the slaves was the self-affirming nature that the spirituals provided:

> Slaves used the spirituals to reveal themselves to each other, and to provide an alternative definition of self that challenged white claims. The spirituals, both in the act of singing and in the words of the songs, became a critical part of countermanding the master's ideology about slaves. This was a form of rhetorical resistance that both limited the slaves' worth to their masters and, more importantly, enabled slaves to refute the very definitions and assumptions on which this psychological oppression was based. As they refuted those definitions, they replaced them with ones of their own making. (Sanger 179)

While Turner benefited from both the storytelling and singing to help shape his oratory, it was primarily the oratorical style of black preaching that gave his rhetoric its power. The type of sermon that Turner heard when he was young came from a preacher named Isaac Cook, who lived in Turner's hometown of Newberry Courthouse. Little is known of Cook, but reports of his preaching note that he was a very "eloquent and persuasive speaker, and that he was looked upon by all as a great man" (Angell, *Black Methodist* 93).

A white man named "Luther" offered a brief synopsis of a sermon that Cook delivered. Cook's text was Jonah 1:6; *"What meanest thou O sleeper, arise and call upon thy God."* Luther wrote:

> His description of a sinner in the ark of carnal security, afloat on the storm-tossed ocean of life, in danger of going to the bottom, and yet asleep and unconscious of peril, was to my boyish mind indescribably awful. I left the place where the sermon was preached under an irresistible conviction that I had listened to a man of God, and the best thing I could do for myself was to take warning, and seek for refuge in Christ as I had been so faithfully exhorted to do. (Angell, *Black Methodist* 94)

If the account given is correct, then we can glean some facts from this sermon. First, one can see that Cook did not take a "literal" interpretive position on the text. The text speaks of Jonah being asleep on the ship while a storm is brewing. The captain of the ship wakes Jonah, and in essence, wonders why he is asleep and tells him to wake up and "call on his God" for help.

However, instead of just recounting the story, Cook went *beneath the text,* and extrapolated a *spiritual* meaning for his audience. He symbolically labeled the audience as Jonah; the boat symbolized the false security that carnal desires provide; the storm became the trials we face in life. Jonah symbolically represents sinners who need saving.

This experiential rhetorical style of preaching fascinated a young Turner. Angell, in his biography of Turner, notes that Turner and his childhood friends loved "imitating preachers" and "baptizing" each other. Some of Turner's "earliest sermons were addressed to the family cow in the pasture" (Angell, *Bishop* 9).

While imitating preachers might have been a form of play for Turner and his friends, Turner did feel a call to "lead" people at a young age. Angell noted that when Turner was twelve years old, he dreamed that "millions of people would come to him for instruction and that he would teach them while standing on a mountain" (Angell, *Bishop* 9). This, along with the earlier dream he had at eight or nine years old, cause Turner to conclude early on in his life that God had something special for him to do. No doubt, this form of play spilled over into Turner's dreams.

However, it was at the Israel AME Church that Turner began to understand the difference between a *speech* and an *oration.* Author and historian Kenneth Greenberg, in studying Southern oratory, noted the difference between the two when he wrote:

> Speeches can have many different forms and purposes. They can be used to inform an audience or to arouse it to action. They can be used to subtly persuade or viciously to malign. Orations, in terms of their content, can also be used for these purposes, often making them hard to distinguish from speeches. What is

different about an oration was that one of its primary functions was to *inspire respect, even awe for the speaker in the minds of the listeners. An oration, in contrast to a speech, was the public display of a superior personality.* Orations allowed statesmen to display their independence, as well as their superior intelligence and virtue. (12, emphasis mine)

Drawing from Greenberg, one notices an *ethos-driven function* of the oration. In other words, what orations tend to do is to create an air of credibility and respect for the speaker. In addition, if Greenberg is correct, the oration depends even more on *delivery*. What the speaker wants to do with an oration is to create a *persona through performance* that would create a "superior personality." Ponton wrote, "He used a great many gestures. He had the magnetism of an orator. He could entertain his audience for hours at a time. He was persuasive and eloquent . . . and he was never without an engagement to perform some useful service, not only to his own church but to all churches and his race in general . . ." (128). Turner's elocution and delivery established him as a leader not only within the confines of the AME Church, but also as a leader of national notoriety. In short, befriending powerful politicians and preaching at a prominent church in the nation's capitol would not have meant anything if Turner could not deliver an oration.

Turner's public career lasted over sixty years—and while a fuller, more deeper analysis of his rhetoric deserves attention, I do not take up that work here. I examine Turner's career from 1866-1895. My goal is to demonstrate how Turner's rhetorical trajectory shifted throughout his career—moving from someone who was optimistic about the prospects of African Americans and America in general immediately after the Civil War, to one who was pessimistic about the prospects of African Americans and America near the end of his life. I do this by offering a close reading of four speech texts of Turner—two early in his career and two later. Each speech text makes up a chapter and my central argument is that Henry McNeal Turner adopted a prophetic persona and used prophetic rhetoric to move, transform, encourage, uplift, and challenge his audiences. In the concluding chapter, I offer a brief examination of Turner's career after 1895, a summary of my findings, and Turner's place within the prophetic tradition. It is my hope that in examining Turner by weaving both text and context together for analysis, this exercise will become a springboard for further understanding and study on one of the most important figures in American public address in the nineteenth century.

Notes

1. For more information on African Americans and Lyceums, see Angela Ray's *The Lyceum and Public Culture in the Nineteenth Century United States*

and Shirley Wilson Logan's *Liberating Language: Sites of Rhetorical Education in Nineteenth Century Black America.*

2. For an overview of Turner's legislative agenda, see the MA thesis of Elbert Martin, *The Life of Henry McNeal Turner, 1834-1870.*

3. While Turner did not have any children with his subsequent wives, sources say that Turner and his first wife Eliza had as many as fourteen children with only two surviving into adulthood. Several of their other children could have died pre-birth or died days after birth. Turner was silent on this issue. However, in commemorating the anniversary of Eliza's death, Turner mentions the deaths of Eliza's mother, his mother, and "the babes who went a little before her to the heavenly land." See *Bishop H.M. Turner Upon the Anniversary of his Wife's Death* in the *Christian Recorder*, 31 July 1890.

4. J. Minton Batten, "Henry M. Turner, Negro Bishop Extraordinary," *Church History* 7.3 (1938): 231-246.

5. Edwin S. Redkey, "Bishop Turner's African Dream," *The Journal of American History* 54.2 (1967): 271-290; Jane Herndon, "Henry McNeal Turner's African Dream: A Re-Evaluation," *Mississippi Quarterly* (1969); Edwin S. Redkey, *Respect Black: Speeches and Writings of Henry McNeal Turner* (1971); Josephus Coan, "Henry McNeal Turner: A Fearless Prophet of Black Liberation," *Journal of the Inter-Denominational Theological Center (ITC)* (1973).

6. Edwin S. Redkey, "Rocked in the Cradle of Consternation: A Black Chaplain in the Union Army Reports on the Struggle to Take Fort Fisher, North Carolina, in the Winter of 1864-1865," *American Heritage* 31 (1980): 70-79.

7. Melbourne Cummings, "The Rhetoric of Bishop Henry McNeal Turner: Leading Advocate in the African Emigration Movement, 1866-1907," diss. University of California at Los Angeles, 1972; Andre E. Johnson, "The Prophetic Oratory of Henry McNeal Turner," diss. University of Memphis, 2008; Melbourne S. Cummings, "The Rhetoric of Bishop Henry McNeal Turner," *Journal of Black Studies* 12 (1982): 457-470; Richard W. Leeman, "Speaking as Jeremiah: Henry McNeal Turner's I Claim the Rights of a Man," *Howard Journal of Communications* 17 (2006): 223-243.

8. This is changing. Many rhetorical critics are moving to some textual analysis that focuses on what the rhetor invited the audience to do.

9. This is debatable. For example, one could make a strong case that Turner's emigration rhetoric did provide the impetus for the Great Migration Northward of African Americans from the South.

10. The "traditions" of African American social and political thought vary. For instance, Brotz lists emigration, assimilation, and cultural and political nationalism, while West lists exceptionalist, assimilationist, marginalist, and humanist traditions. Of these, I would also add the intergrationalist and economic nationalist traditions. These traditions and/or thoughts are responses from African Americans to their marginal status in America. For more information on

these traditions, see Howard Brotz, *African American Social and Political Thought 1850-1920* (New Brunswick, NJ: Transaction Publishers, 1993) and Cornel West, *Prophesy Deliverence: An Afro-American Revolutionary Christianity*, Anniversary ed. (Louisville, KY: Westminister John Knox Press, 2002).

11. For example see Robert Branham and W. Barnett Pearce, "Between Text and Context: Toward a Rhetoric of Contextual Reconstruction," *Quarterly Journal of Speech* 71 (1985): 19-36 and Leah Ceccarelli, *Shaping Science with Rhetoric: The Cases of Dobzhansky, Schrodinger and Wilson* (Chicago: University of Chicago Press, 2001).

12. See "Will We Have Ears to Hear: The African American Prophetic Tradition in the Age of Obama" *The African American Pulpit* (Spring 2010) and "The Prophetic Persona of James Cone and the Rhetorical Theology of Black Theology," vol. 8.3.

13. There has been some discrepancy in the actual year of Turner's birth. See Stephen Ward Angell's *Bishop Henry McNeal Turner and African American Religion in the South,* footnote on page 278.

14. On African Americans being self-taught in the nineteenth century, see Shirley Wilson Logan's *Sites of Rhetorical Education in Nineteenth-Century Black America*, especially chapter 2.

Chapter One

"Let By-Gones be By-Gones": Emancipation and Turner's Celebratory Prophecy

When Henry McNeal Turner stood in the pulpit at Springfield Baptist Church and gave the Emancipation Day address on January 1, 1866 in Augusta, Georgia, he had already established quite a name for himself. He had already preached integrated revivals, served at the most prominent AME church (Israel AME Church in Washington, D.C.), befriended several powerful and influential members of Congress, and most of all, wrote numerous letters, articles, and essays to the *Christian Recorder* newspaper. Already by this time, many throughout the AME Church knew of Turner. However, Turner's notoriety expanded when he became the first African American chaplain commissioned in the Union Army.

Turner's selection as the first African American chaplain garnered mention from the *New York Times*. The *Times* thought that the selection of Turner was "worthily bestowed" since Turner "labored assiduously for the elevation of his race" ("Colored Chaplain" 11-14-63). The praise continued for Turner as *Harper's Weekly* ran a feature, which also included a portrait and provided probably one of the earliest bio sketches of the preacher ("Rev. H.M. Turner" 12-13-63). However, while serving in the military, it was Turner's letters to the *Christian Recorder* newspaper that help establish his prophetic persona.

Turner's letters from the battlefield attracted many readers—both black and white and both in the North and South (Redkey, "Henry McNeal Turner" 336). While as Redkey notes, "there is no precise measure of the circulation of the Recorder," the newspaper still was influential because many of the AME "preachers drew on their articles for sermons and lectures" (340). Moreover, someone typically would read the newspaper aloud to many congregants and people who could not read and they would share what they heard through the informal church grapevine.

Turner's rhetoric in those letters to the *Christian Recorder* has not received much scholarly attention. They not only informed African Americans and others about the war and described many of the battles in exhilarating detail, but also helped establish Turner as a public figure. In addition to writing about the war, Turner also focused his attention on church matters. He promoted the merger of the AME and AME Zion Churches, challenged AME ministers to contribute to the *Recorder* more often, and wrote glowingly about the growth of the AME Church after the end of the Civil War. In addition to traveling with his regiment and ducking "bombs and balls flying around his head," Turner also found the time to write glowing eulogies of departed friends, to chastise civilian men against making advances to women whose husbands were at war, and to celebrate how black soldiers clamored to learn how to read. This would lead Turner to call for more books and newspapers for the soldiers to read.[1]

However, his public persona took on a prophetic one as well. It was never lost on Turner that he was a Union Army chaplain and though Turner lobbied fiercely for the position, he believed God called him to this duty. He never forgot that he was a minister of the gospel and had a duty to speak up and speak out on issues important to him and his fellow soldiers. In a private letter to the Secretary of War, Edwin Stanton, Turner demanded that he let him know "ONCE FOR ALL whether it is the intention of the government to have colored chaplains or not" (Turner, Aug. 1, 1863). In another, tired of the disrespect he faced while ministering to sick and injured soldiers, he asked for some "badge or mark," on his uniform that would have designated him as a chaplain (Turner, June 30, 1864).

While Turner would avail himself to the private letter when asking or demanding something he felt he deserved, he saved most of his prophetic fire for the newspapers. After describing a battle in which he proclaimed that his regiment "carried the day," Turner, noting even white soldier support, critiqued the government for not paying black soldiers their full pay and warned of a day of reckoning.

And the universal expression among the white soldiers was, *That it is a burning shame for Government to keep these men out of their full pay.* Indeed, many of the white soldiers of the Battery actually cursed and swore about the Government not paying the colored troops their full pay. And I would here remark, and I do not care if Congress and the entire administration see the remark, *that unless the colored troops get their full pay very soon, I tremble with fear for the issue of things.* The tardiness of Congress in this matter has been watched by the colored soldiers with an undying eagerness, and every paper is ransacked with a view to their pay. But God grant that the evil may be speedily remedied, is all I will now say (Johnson, An African American Pastor, Vol. 2, 22, emphasis original).

He aimed his invectives sometimes at the Union soldiers as well. In writing about the killing of Confederate prisoners of war Turner wrote,

There is one thing, though, which is highly endorsed by an immense number of both white and colored people, which I am sternly opposed to, and that is, the killing of all the rebel prisoners taken by our soldiers. True, the rebels have set the example, particularly in killing the colored soldiers; but it is a cruel one, and two cruel acts never make one humane act. Such a course of warfare is an outrage upon civilization and nominal Christianity. And inasmuch as it was presumed that we would carry out a brutal warfare, let us disappoint our malicious anticipators, by showing the world that higher sentiments not only prevail, but actually predominate. (Johnson, An African American Pastor, Vol. 2, 29-30).

Turner also found time to respond to political matters. In a letter to the editor published September 17, 1864, Turner commented on the *Chicago Platform* of the Democratic Party during the 1864 presidential election.

The infamous catalogue of principles, embodied in that infernal instrument, called the Chicago platform, the framers of which out to everyone be hung, till dead by the neck, or shot till riddled like Napoleon's lion, has not affected the determined conclusion to strike down the last foe to the American flag, and her free institutions. Who would have thought that an American heart, could have been so perverted at this stage of events, as to publicly endorse such audacious resolution as those incarnate devils at Chicago formed, as the basis of a Presidential campaign? They are enough to revolt human modesty, and turn our most prudish promptings into confusion and burning shame. Never let the American people, in all coming time, stand aghast at any thing again. ("Johnson, An African American Pastor: Vol. 2, 42)

Later in the same letter, Turner openly criticizes President Lincoln for his lethargic attitude towards people who would only want him and his presidency to fail.

Had the President from the beginning administered the stern mandates of moral and political justice to the enemies of the country. . . . The evil they are now perpetrating and the injury they are doing the Government, in its efforts to crush the rebellion, would have been entirely obviated. . . . The argument, that Mr. Lincoln was obliged to court the affections of the Democratic parties, to secure the co-operation of the whole North, is nothing more than a farce. The principles which should have governed him, were those of eternal justice; they were clearly laid down in the Bible, and engraved upon the tables of nature; they were throbbed in every pulsation of the human heart, and preached by the proclamation of John C. Fremont, in the opening of the war. And had these principles been his modus operandi, or his compass, to run the national ship by, amid the stormy winds, and lurid siege of war, this opposition party would have set in profound dumbness, until the last foe had bitten the dust at his lordly feet. But instead thereof, they rise with indignant majesty before him, contemning, insulting, and trying to defame . . . . (Johnson, An African American Pastor: Vol. 2, 44)

However, Turner saw the hand of God in all of this. While he believed the nation was passing through a "terrible revolution" that would "purge her from the dross of base corruption," he also believed that God in God's own providence would work this out for good. However, he did not stop there. He also suggested that human agency was also involved in turning bad things into good and anything else was to "acknowledge the existence of the devil as important as the existence of God, in the scale of physical and moral elevation" (Johnson, An African American Pastor: Vol. 2, 43).

After the Civil War, Turner's letters focused on the newfound relationships between blacks and whites in the South. He also focused on recruiting newly emancipated blacks to join the United States Army, as well as seeing that the freed people had churches of their own. However, much of his writing centered on reporting the condition of newly freed people. While assigned in North Carolina, Turner lamented on the conditions of the formerly enslaved people.

We found thousands of colored people on the eve of starvation, while the parties authorized by the government to issue rations were cheating, stealing, and defrauding them of their lawful subsistence. We found hundreds of colored men with scraps of paper in their pockets, as the only reward for one and two years work, performed under the promise of being paid by the government, while the money had actually been drawn, and lavished upon the greasy carcasses of lazy thieves and their accomplices. (Johnson, An African American Pastor: Vol. 2, 138)

In response to this and building upon the government's work with the Freedmen's Bureau, Turner called for the government to hire black preachers and lecturers to travel the South to assist the newly emancipated people. Turner suggested that the people needed teaching in the areas of "virtue, chastity, honor, the value of a promise made, the contemptibleness [sic] of dishonesty and indolence." He argued that the former enslaved people needed "instruction in everything, and especially the little things of life, such points of attention as thousands would never stoop to surmise" (Johnson, An African American Pastor: Vol. 2, 149). Turner, however, was quick to note that he was not labeling all the freed people as ignorant. He claimed that some of the "best historians, orators and architects had been slaves in the South." Nevertheless, he believed that these were exceptions and that the majority of the Southern blacks needed help after the many years of slavery.

When Turner arrived in Augusta, Georgia in December of 1865, he had much on his mind. He had a job as a chaplain with the Freedmen's Bureau, yet his heart pulled him to focus more on his church work. He believed he could do both, but as the demands grew, with the resignation of James Lynch and the death of William Gaines, local church leaders in Georgia, Turner decided to resign his chaplaincy position and turn his complete focus to the church. When Turner arrived, the churches and many of the people that Turner met were in disarray. He intended to focus his attention on helping the freed people establish themselves in the "new South," while at the same time building the AME Church. However, the Emancipation Day celebration was on the horizon and the officials needed a keynote speaker. Who better fit the bill than Rev. Henry McNeal Turner?

Officials called this Emancipation Day the *First Anniversary of Freedom* because this was the first New Year's day after the end of slavery. Emancipation Day celebrations started in 1808 when America officially ended the Atlantic slave trade.[2] It was on January 1, 1808 that Northern blacks came together to celebrate this event by singing and hearing speeches on freedom. On July 4, 1827, however, the state of New York abolished slavery, and blacks there had a new day on which to celebrate. New Yorkers were not alone in this celebration. History records that five other states adopted July 4 as their "Emancipation Day" (which eventually changed to July 5) and soon other states celebrated on July 5 as well.

In 1834, blacks replaced the July 5 celebration when enslaved Africans in the West British Isles found liberation on August 1, and that date became the new day to celebrate emancipation.[3] While these West Indies Emancipation Days were similar to the earlier celebrations, there were two major differences. First, many whites joined with blacks to celebrate this emancipation and secondly, since the crowds for many of these celebrations were huge, the celebrations moved away from black churches and were held outdoors. This led to a more festive celebration with parades during the day and emancipation balls at night.

Regardless of the dates and times of celebration, emancipation days placed emphasis on four themes. First, the "explicit rationale" for the celebration was the call to remember—to remember and appreciate the day of freedom as well as remembering those who were still enslaved. Second, there was a call to unity. Many speakers admonished blacks to "identify with each other" and to hold "high standards of conduct in order not to provoke charges of immorality or irresponsibility upon the race" (Gravely 307). Third, there was identification with Africa along with "romanticized pictures of the continent prior to the coming of the white European" (Gravely 307). Speakers at these celebrations often used the terms "Ethiopian" or "Sons of Africa" when speaking about black people. However, even this identification with Africa was qualified somewhat with an acknowledgment and appreciation of the fact that speakers and members of the audiences were born in America.

Finally, and most significantly, these speeches required black orators to explain slavery. Thus, speakers who declared the black race as powerful, intelligent, and able to live in freedom also had to ask why God would allow slavery in the first place. While there were many different answers and reasons given, the one that gained the most support was to leave the question unresolved in the mystery of God's providence.

How did black speakers get across their messages or, in other words, what type of rhetoric was used at these events? Wilson Moses argues that black orators adopted the jeremiad tradition and developed what he calls the *"black jeremiad."* For Moses, the black jeremiad described "The constant warnings issued by blacks to whites, concerning the judgment that was to come for slavery" (*Black Messiahs* 30-31).

> The black jeremiad was mainly a pre-Civil war phenomenon and showed the traditional preoccupation with impending doom. It was often directed at a white audience and it bemoaned the sinfulness of slaveholders—fellow Americans who defied the natural and divine law that they were covenantally bound to uphold—and predicted God's punishment that was to come. (Moses, *Black Messiahs* 31)

It was within this prophetic tradition that Turner delivered his 1866 Emancipation Day speech. However, while many of the themes in Turner's speech were reminiscent of Emancipation Day speeches, this speech was different because the rhetorical situation had changed and his use of the traditional black jeremiad would be of no use. The Civil War was over, and the Union had prevailed. While debate about the meaning, purpose, and significance of the war did not end, among blacks there was one undisputed and certain point—the war ended slavery and ultimately set black people free. While many whites regarded the war as struggle to preserve the Union, blacks saw it as a war of liberation.

Moreover, the Thirteenth Amendment had become part of the Constitution. Passed by Congress on January 31, 1865, and ratified by the states on December 18, 1865, the amendment prohibited "slavery and involuntary servitude in the United States and gave Congress authority to enforce the prohibition" (Nieman 56). For blacks, this meant total freedom. For the first time in the history of America, slavery and involuntary servitude were against the law.

The Great Christmas Insurrection Scare of 1865 also complicated the context of Turner's speech. Although proven a hoax, the rumors among whites that former slaves planned a rebellion during the Christmas holidays proved persuasive. By November of 1865, the insurrection rhetoric had spread to more than sixty counties and half dozen parishes throughout the South, none more so than near Augusta, Georgia in Watkinsville (Carter 348).

It was against this backdrop that Henry McNeal Turner spoke to a primarily black audience to celebrate the first year of Emancipation.[4] Also in the audience that day were whites, many who represented the Freedmen's Bureau and who were officers in the Union Army. Redkey wrote that since Turner was a "black officer (chaplain) and a preacher, he was the logical candidate to address the Emancipation Day Anniversary Celebration" at "a time when there was confusion in the South over what the federal policy toward the ex-confederate states would be" (*Respect* 5).

The four-part speech includes an introduction, in which Turner compares this day of celebration to other days of celebration. He also addresses America's divinely inspired covenant agreement with God. In the second and longest part of the speech, Turner switches from the moment of celebration to talk about the horrors and meaning of slavery and black heroism in the Civil War. Third, Turner outlines eight "freedoms" that both blacks and whites can celebrate together as they move forward in harmony together. Finally, in the conclusion, Turner prophetically charges blacks to be men and charges both blacks and whites to get along in this new era of freedom.

Turner's Emancipation Day Speech

Introduction

Turner starts his speech by sharing the real situation and directly considering the occasion:

> Gentlemen and Ladies, or Fellow Citizens, I should have said, we have assembled to-day under circumstances, unlike those of any other day in the history of our lives. We have met for the purpose of celebrating this, the first day of the New Year, not because it is the first New Year's day we ever saw, but because it is the first one we ever enjoyed. O! how different this day from similar days of the past. The first day of January hitherto, was one of gloom and fearful suspense. The foundation of our social comforts hung upon the scales of apprehension, and fate with its decisions of weal and woe looked every one of us in the face, and dread forebodings kept in dubious agitation, every fleeting moment that passed. But to-day we stand upon such a sandy foundation. Uncertainty is no more the basis of our existence; we have for our fulcrum the eternal principles of right and equity. (*Celebration* 4)

According to Turner, the reason for the celebration this year was that blacks finally were "citizens." By correcting his salutation and adding "fellow citizens," Turner announced to his audience, both black and white, that he considers himself and his fellow blacks to be "citizens." This opening move connected Turner to a reversal of the *rhetoric of place*. Kirt Wilson has argued that after slavery and with the start of Reconstruction, Southern conservatives adopted this strategy "to counteract the Republican's agenda and resurrected an old idea, the notion of place, to create "a rhetoric that maintained the appearance of reconstruction while it reaffirmed disparate power relations between African and European Americans" (xv).

The rhetoric of place was common in white Southern discourse of the time. An example appeared in the language of then vice president Andrew Johnson when he spoke at a Knoxville unionist meeting in 1864:

> The government of the United States and the governments of the States . . . *are*
> *the governments of the free white man*, and to be controlled and administered
> by him, and the negro [sic] must assume the status (place) to which the laws of
> an enlightened, moral and high-toned society shall assign him. (Cimprich 189,
> emphasis original)

By defining the government of the United States as the government of the
"free white man," Johnson *places* whites in charge and assumes that whites
should control and administer the government. Moreover, beyond this political
arrangement, he implies that all blacks must assume the status (place) assigned,
and it is notable that Johnson is not *assigning the place to blacks*, but it is "enlightened, moral and high-toned society" that enforces this hierarchy. Therefore,
by arguing for separate stations in public life Johnson and other whites must
assume the duties of leadership in government and society while blacks must
adopt a passive and subordinate position. Since no one knows what these duties
are, this rhetoric assumes that "high-toned society," by some natural process,
will discover the place for black people.

Knowing that white Southerners employed a rhetoric of place, Turner
(re)*placed* black people as citizens. After the Civil War, with the Confederacy
destroyed and Georgia still not readmitted to the Union, there was technically no
foundation or framework to claim citizenship—for blacks *or whites*. In other
words, no one could call herself or himself a citizen of any place. However, that
did not stop whites from believing that they were free citizens because, at the
least, they could claim that others had not enslaved them. With the passage of
the Thirteenth Amendment, it opened an avenue for blacks to claim citizenship
privileges as well.

Therefore, in the opening of his speech, Turner equated citizenship with
freedom and/or being free. By placing blacks within the bounds of citizenship,
blacks now could "assemble" "under circumstances unlike those of any other
day of our lives" (*Celebration* 4). For Turner and other blacks in the audience
the term citizen helped erase the "gloom and fearful suspense" that was associated with January 1. However, what were those gloomy and suspenseful mo-
ments? Turner acknowledges them later in the speech:

> This day which hitherto separated so many families and tear wet so many faces;
> heaved so many hearts and filled the air with so many groans and sighs; this of
> all others the most bitter day of the year to our poor miserable race, shall hence-
> forth and forever be filled with acclamations of the wildest joy, and expressions
> of ecstasy too numerous for angelic pens to write. (*Celebration* 4)

Here Turner alluded to the separation of loved ones that took place within
enslaved communities all over the South. Usually on January 1, with families
separated at the whim of their owners, many never saw their loved ones again.
During the days of slavery, many slaves gathered on New Year's Eve for celebration and lamentation in churches and the "brush harbors" all over the South

awaiting the day of separation. However, for Turner, this New Year's Day marks a redemptive moment. Turner considered what this redemption was and how it happened in the next portion of the speech.

America as Divinely Inspired

Next, Turner appropriated the doctrine of the sacred mission of America. As he continued to celebrate this day by comparing it with other celebrations, Turner shifted his attention to the Fourth of July. The Day of Independence was important in Turner's narrative because not only did America declare independence from English colonialism, but also it was the moment when America discovered its true mission in the world. Speaking about July 4 and the Declaration of Independence, Turner declared:

> The white people have made it a day of gratitude and general rejoicing ever since 1776 . . . because on that day they threw off the British Yoke and trampled under foot the scepter of despotic tyranny. They raised the standard of independence on that ever memorable day and every man rallied to its support by the Declaration of Independence. . . . As soon as every name of that august assembly convened within was appended to that mighty document, which has ever since defied the world, a little boy shouted out "ring, ring"! and with all the power of a freeman, he struck that bell one hundred blows, (the same number of days it took Abraham Lincoln to smelt out the bell of liberty from September 22nd, 1862, to January 1st, 1863) and the bell in response chimed out the irons words engraved upon its rim, "Proclaim liberty throughout the land, and to the inhabitants thereof" and thus the stone cut out of the mountain without hands, as seen by the ancient king, make its first revolution towards filling the whole world, as was predicted, for I hold that America and her Democratic principles and institutions is the great stone which is spoken of by the prophet Daniel. (*Celebration* 6)

This passage grounded Turner's rhetoric in the belief that America was divinely inspired to "proclaim liberty throughout the land." However, he also added scriptural authority from the biblical book of Daniel, and he equated "America and her Democratic principles and institutions" with that "great stone spoken in the book of Daniel." The "divine mission" of the country requires the abolition of inequality (slavery) that the "democratic principles and institutions" promoted. This is why Turner can later proclaim, "God seemed to have held it (America) back for some important purpose" (*Celebration* 7). This purpose of America, divinely inspired and proclaimed in the book of Daniel, was for America to promote equality not only at home, but also throughout the whole world.

The myth of a "Chosen Nation" was nothing new to American oratorical discourse.[5] Already present in early Puritan thought, it drew from the Old Testament notion of Israel being "chosen," and it claimed that a group of people (in this case America) is "chosen" by God for a specific purpose. Drawing from this myth, Turner used the divine mission of America as a basis for adopting a prophetic persona and thereby spoke prophetically about a wide range of issues starting with slavery and the meaning of the Civil War.

Slavery and the Civil War

Prophetic Reinterpretation of Slavery

By defining America through its association with biblical prophecy and assigning the nation's "divine mission" to promote equality throughout the world, Turner constructed a rhetorical problem for himself—the same problem that confronted many nineteenth-century African American orators and social thinkers—the problem of slavery. How can Turner explain slavery if America was divinely inspired by the "prayers of the Puritans" and "founded upon free principles and recognizing equality in all men" (*Celebration* 6-7)? Turner found his answer through a prophetic reinterpretation of the institution. He began this effort by maintaining that:

> The African was, I have no doubt, committed to the care of the white man as a trust from God. That he should clear up the land and pioneer the march of civilization by agricultural labor and domestic pursuits is a fact about which I have no hesitancy in admitting. That the white man should have made him work and exacted so much daily toil as was commensurate with the necessities of life and the developments of the nation's resources was all in keeping with order and sense, for he was by virtue of his superior advantages thereby his superior in intellect and the guardian of the negro. (*Celebration* 8)

For Turner, Africans were committed to the *trust of the white man*. Turner probably used *trust* here as a person who holds title to property for the benefit of another. Therefore, in saying that the "African was committed to the trust of the white man," Turner in effect defines the African as property and makes the white person the trustee.

Moreover, Turner maintained that the *trust* itself did not come from humans; it came from God, thus making it a *sacred trust* between God and white people. The African did not have a voice in the arrangement. The African was to "clear up the land" and "pioneer the march of civilization" by agricultural and domestic labor. In other words, whites were supposed to be the leaders and caretakers of the trust, and the Africans were to do the work and provide the labor to build the country.

Turner probably formed this type of interpretation of slavery years earlier from arguments he heard from apologists for the institution. While one of the most prominent arguments against slavery was that it was morally wrong for one human to own another human, pro-slavery activists countered that slave owners did not own the slave as a person, *but owned the right to a slave's labor*. Presbyterian minister James Henley Thornwell articulated this position when he stated, "The property of man in man is only the property of man in human toil. The laborer becomes capital, not because he is a thing, but because he is the exponent of a presumed labor" (Jenkins 109). This rhetorical strategy separated humans from their labor. Since the labor was in fact the only thing slave owners bought, they indeed had a right to it as property. The fact that the labor came with a body attached was immaterial.

Turner's interpretation of slavery, while sounding conciliatory, was in fact very radical. By appropriating a "pro-slavery argument," Turner then could prophetically critique the argument by offering a reinterpretation of this "sacred trust."

> But that the white man should bar all avenues of improvement and hold the Black man as he would a horse or cow; deface the image of God by ignorance, which the black man was the representative of, was the crime which offended Heaven. We gave the white man our labor, yes! Every drop of sweat which oozed from our face he claimed as his own. In return, he should have educated us, taught us to read and write, at least, and to have seen that Africa was well supplied with missionaries. (*Celebration* 8)

Turner rejected the argument that slave owners only purchased the labor from enslaved people. The labor came from humans who are not like a "horse or cow" because unlike horses and cows, blacks can improve their stations or status in life. Nevertheless, there was a problem with this sacred trust. Whites barred all avenues of improvement and in so doing, they "defaced the image of God" by causing "ignorance" to the black race. What whites should have done with the sacred trust from God was to teach the slaves how to read, write, and at least send missionaries to Africa.

Framed this way, Turner placed whites in a position of sin. The sin of whites was the breaking of the sacred trust. Whites not only did not educate enslaved people, but whites also did not educate Africans by sending missionaries to the continent. In other words, whites were sinful because of their lack of commitment to the intellect of the enslaved person.

This is an especially important point because one of the rhetorical strategies of white apologists for slavery was that whites were pure, moral, and righteous, while blacks were dark, evil, and sinful. Many argued that slavery was in fact humane for Africans because then they could learn Christianity (Smith 152).

However, Turner *replaced* this image with one of failure:

> Had the (white) ministers exhausted half their learning and study in showing the white people their duty to the negro as a trust from God that they have in trying to prove the divine right of slavery, Africa would have been two-thirds civilized today and the nation twice as wealthy, and the bones of a million of our countrymen would not now lie bleaching over every Southern State. (*Celebration* 8)

When white people broke the trust with God, terrible consequences ensued. While white people tried to prove the "divine right of slavery," they failed not only their duty to God, but also their duty to African Americans. Moreover, even though Africa was already wealthy, it should have been twice as wealthy and "two thirds civilized" had whites done their duty. Finally, had whites done their duty to God and black people, there would not have been "bones bleaching over every Southern state." In other words, Turner argued that the cause and the results of war arose from the failure of whites to do their duty.

Framed this way, Turner declared:

> Had the white people treated slavery as a trust from God, it would never have ended in a terrible war. . . . But the way it was treated, and the ends in which it was appropriated, was an insult to God. And nothing less than floods of his burning ire and the thunders of his scathing judgment, poured out on the *guilty heads of the violators of this law*, and crimsoned acres of ground with the heart's gore of tens of thousands, could satisfy divine justice and make slavery despicable in the eyes of a country which had loved it so dearly and nurtured it so long. Men, yes—men of every rank and position—had become darkened to the true *status of manhood*, because worldly gain lay at the bottom of all his moral considerations. (*Celebration* 9)

Through a reinterpretation of proslavery arguments, Turner has *placed* blacks as citizens and *displaced* whites from their position of moral superiority. Whites failed as caregivers of the sacred trust and whites had "insulted God" by failing to perform their duty to educate black people. Therefore, God had to exact judgment, not on everybody, but only on the "guilty heads of the violators of this law." More specifically, Turner referred to slave owners and ministers who failed as caregivers. However, to what law did Turner refer? He referred to the trust God gave white people to care for the African. God had to exact judgment because whites failed to see Africans as the "image of God" and continually defaced that image by enslaving them.

Turner believed that the judgment God exacted for the sin of slavery was the Civil War itself. However, for Turner the war had two purposes. The war satisfied God's divine justice, and made slavery so despicable in the eyes of a country which had "loved it so dearly and nurtured it so long." Therefore, for Turner, the war became an apocalyptic moment that enabled the country to see the evils of slavery and to understand how the country strayed from its divine purpose.

However, Turner also did something else. Framed again this way, Turner affirmed the long-held Christian concept that God made all humans in the image of God. Therefore, when whites did not honor the sacredness of their charge and removed blacks from their place, it was not only an insult and disgrace to the image of God, it also defamed God.

In addition, the "image of God" language served another function. It placed whites and blacks together as sisters and brothers. Whites had little difficulty believing they were in the image of God—but to say blacks were the image of God was to say both blacks and whites had the same origin and beginnings.

Turner placed both black and whites as equals not necessarily under secular law, but under God.

Moreover, Turner argued that whites broke the "sacred trust" with God because of a "desire for worldly gain" (*Celebration* 9), thereby moving from the sacred to the profane. This also allowed Turner to highlight the real motive behind slavery—economics. It was economics and not the idea of being a committed caregiver of the African that justified slavery and made it disreputable. In short, Turner prophetically revealed slavery's real motive—money—and this insight led Turner later to demand reparations for blacks for the free labor they gave to help build America.

However, one question lingers—why the need for slavery at all? Turner addressed that question and grounded his answer in the *divine mission of America*. When speaking on the introduction of the slave trade in America Turner explains:

> The early settlers of this country had run from outrage themselves and had manifested a desire to civilize the heathen and to build up an asylum for the oppressed of all nations and to enact laws, which would contemplate justice to all men. *Therefore, God seeing the African stand in need of civilization* sanctioned for a while the slave trade *not that it was in harmony with his fundamental laws for one man to rule another, nor did God ever contemplate that the Negro was to be reduced to the status of a vassal,* but as a subject of moral and intellectual culture. *So God winked or lidded his eyeballs at the institution of slavery as a test of the white man's obedience, and elevation of the Negro.* (*Celebration* 8, emphasis mine)

Turner believed that America was a place for the oppressed of all nations to come and gain civilization as well as enjoy the fruits of justice, and this belief explained slavery—it was necessary for civilization of the African.[6] Slavery, however, was not ever in harmony with God's fundamental laws; neither did God mean for blacks forever to be in a state of servitude. The African was to be a subject (student) for a while to achieve a higher moral and intellectual culture.

However flawed Turner's view of slavery is from our current perspective, we need to appreciate the subtlety of his rhetorical maneuver. He redefined slavery in terms of what slavery should have been, and he emphasized the distance between its legitimate goal, a test of the white man's fidelity to God's mission, and what it actually became, a suppression of the divine nature of a people for economic gain. White people, in the spirit of the "early settlers" (not the founding fathers) should have done God's work, but they failed the obedience test. The War came as retribution for this failure and a correction for its consequence, and the "extremities of two colors, white and black" are now to meet and "embrace each other" and work together to solve this "great problem" for the good of everybody, which now has the "sanction of heaven" (*Celebration* 8).

Therefore, God creates a new covenant with both blacks and whites to do God's work. White people could not do it alone—they tried but failed. Moreover, blacks are responsible for this work, and they were to embrace whites to get it done. Offering this reinterpretation of slavery, Turner includes blacks in the overall covenant tradition of the "early settlers" and ends the white monopoly of the teacher/leader roles. For Turner, what this *New Year* demands is mutual respect and equality.

Prophetic Interpretation of the Civil War

After arguing against the "curse of Noah theory"[7] and offering a brief history lesson, Turner turned his attention towards another testament of citizenship and freedom—black participation in the Civil War:

> But it is useless to prowl through ancient history to prove our manhood; go to the bloody fields that have been redeemed by gallons of the richest blood that ever coursed its way through the veins of man. Ask those bleaching bones which lie strewn around Petersburg and Richmond of my brave regiment; then visit Port Hudson, Fort Wagoner, and a hundred other scenes of carnage where black troops fought, bled, and died, "Why are you here?" and the answer will come loud as thunder, "Give me Liberty or give me Death." That was all they wanted, and it is all we want. . . . When the nation first called upon the colored men to rally its flag, a howl and a whine was raised North and South that, "If you arm the Negroes you can never discipline them; they will be cannibals, killed all the women and children and eat them into the bargain." But at the length the Negroes were armed and Ethiopia stretched forth her hands to God with a musket in them. (*Celebration* 10)

Turner's *history lesson* in form of recall intended to prove "our manhood," and he used "our" here to mean *black people's manhood*, thus identifying with his primarily black audience. Manhood was an important feature in the rhetoric of Turner, and one of the ways Turner determined manhood was referring often to the fact that blacks fought gallantly in the Civil War. To prove the manhood status of blacks, Turner offered the fields that have been "redeemed by the gallons of the richest blood"—meaning that many had died for the cause of the war. However, what was the cause? The cause in Turner estimation was liberty, which he equated with freedom. After quoting Patrick Henry's famous saying, "Give me Liberty or give me Death," he proclaimed it was all that African Americans ever wanted.

However, the manhood reference would have meant something else as well. After losing the war, Foster suggested that Southern (white) men questioned whether the Confederates preserved their manhood in defeat. Robert Dabney reflected on this feeling immediately after the war when he stated in an 1871 speech, "The remnant of survivors, few, subjugated, disheartened, almost despairing, and alas, dishonored" were "subjugated to every influence from without, which can be malignantly devised to sap the foundation of their *manhood*, and degrade them into fit material for slaves" (Foster 29, emphasis mine).

Dabney's view was instructive because he equated subjugation, despair, and dishonor with slavery and a loss of manhood. Therefore, whites of the South believed their manhood was lost and now they felt enslaved. Turner turned the same sensibility into a symmetrically opposed conclusion: Union soldiers, including significant numbers of heroic blacks, defeated the Confederacy, and from this it follows that the "manhood" of blacks was firmly established.

The honor, personal bravery, and loyalty of blacks in the war was crucially important to Turner's argument, and he had reminded his audience that blacks had asserted their manhood even before the Union pledged its loyalty to them.

> They made a flag and threw it against the heavens and bid it to float forever; but every star in it was against us; every stripe against us; the red, white and blue was against us; the nation constitution was against us; yes, every state constitution, every state code, every decision from the Supreme Court, every church was against us; prayer and preaching was against us enough to make us fall out with God himself. And why was it? We had always been loyal. (*Celebration* 8-9)

By invoking the memory of the war in which black soldiers fought gallantly, Turner *replaced* (in the eyes of whites) blacks as men worthy of their manhood and at the same time reinforced doubts in whites' minds about their own manhood.

However, there was another reason for Turner to invoke the war. It helped him set up his narrative account of a war story:

> Twelve hundred of us were placed on a bend of the James River, known as Wilson's landing. Shortly afterwards, Gen. Fitz Hugh Lee came down upon us with twenty-five hundred men. As soon as he drove in pickets, a flag of truce was sent in to demand a surrender of the place or he would take it, and death should be the penalty of our refusal. We, however, defied his army so he opened the contest, which raged in fearful suspense for the space of four hours. He charged us three times and finally left, leaving three hundred dead and wounded on the field. The Negro cannibals (for I was one) went out, took up his wounded, carried them to our hospital, and treated them kindly. *White man, show a better heart.* (*Celebration* 10)

By offering this narrative of his activity in the war, Turner *placed* blacks in the collective memory of the Civil War. After the Civil War, many began to shape and define the meaning of the war in both the North and South. Northerners configured the war as a victory for the North without a black presence (Wilson 87-94). Southerners published defenses of their war effort, telling of their accomplishments in it or conducting memorials and offering eulogies honoring the dead, which all contributed eventually to the development of the "Lost Cause" (Foster 25-46). Through his narrative, Turner reminded his audience about black people's participation in this conflict. If blacks participated, white

Northerners could not take all the credit, and white Southerners had to face the realization that blacks actively helped to defeat them.

However, Turner did something else as well. By invoking the memory of the war and the bravery of black soldiers, Turner reminded his audience who won and who lost the war. At this time, whites in the South mourned and struggled with the fact that they had lost the war, while blacks celebrated their victory because they participated in their own cause for freedom.

By showing gratitude to the "Great Disposer of events" (God), blacks can "celebrate the dawn of liberty and dance for joy at the pledge of its security." Further, Turner noted:

> The oppressed of every nation will join the chorus, and Heaven's great organ will lend it harmony. . . . The heroes of the Union, whose blood was spilt for liberty, shall have fragrant names and precious memories and their noble examples will stand as a monument of honor to inspire the just till the world shall end. (*Celebration* 11)

In using poetic language, which is conventional for prophetic discourse, Turner places the recent events in a much larger context. Turner sees the day when the "oppressed of every nation," backed by "heaven's great organ," would join the chorus because Turner's God is a God of action and justice. In short, for Turner, God is on the side of the oppressed; God hears the cries of the oppressed, and God acts on the side of the oppressed. God, as the "Great Disposer" of events, not only acts within God's own time, but also leaves examples that will "inspire the just" until the end of the world. By framing an interpretation of God this way, Turner claims not only that God is on the side of the oppressed, but also that to be just is also to be on the side of the oppressed. It is the "just" who will look and see that the Union had heroes who shed blood for the liberty of the oppressed and this will continue until the "end of the world."

"Blessings" and "Freedoms"

With the promise of blacks fulfilled, now was the time to celebrate. Turner's audience was free to celebrate America as the "stone cut from the mountain" and to celebrate America's divine mission as one that proclaimed and promoted liberty and freedom. For Turner, there was no need to charge or challenge the people to live up to the covenant. The people were living up to the covenant because in Turner's estimation, God acted on behalf of the oppressed and through the Union victory in the Civil War, the ending of slavery, and leading Congress to pass the Thirteenth Amendment, Turner as *prophet* can see God's handiwork in all that had transpired. In short, since God has acted in this way, God blessed or affirmed the covenant and now Turner and his fellow blacks could take part. There was no need for the black jeremiad because what black Jeremiahs proclaimed has become in Turner's estimation a blessed reality.

It is within this blessed reality that Turner offers "special gratitude to heaven" or reasons to celebrate for the "exit of slavery." While directly aimed at his black audience, it is important to note that the first two are not limited to them. Since Turner adopted a prophetic persona of a *covenant prophet*, namely one who represents the covenant and sees all people under the covenant as equal "citizens," the "blessings" must benefit and be shared by everyone.

The first blessing named was the "privilege of meeting as other people." Here Turner explicitly talked about blacks and their inability to meet "without being under the supervision of some white man." Blacks were "watched, feared, and suspicioned [sic]" and when three colored men made a threat, "five hundred white men would rush to arms." Now Turner argued black people could meet without this fear. However, whites also could celebrate because they "can rest quietly, have no fears of being murdered, nor have they to sit up all night; no patrol duty and no fears of us running away." Turner calls this a burden on white people and they should "thank God" that neither party has to watch the other, "but all can attend to their own business" (*Celebration* 12).

What Turner did here in the naming of his first blessing was to proclaim trust between both blacks and whites. During slavery, there was skepticism and distrust among blacks and whites because the system of slavery promoted such animosity. However, since God lifted the burdens off both blacks and whites, now both groups could live out what it means to be truly free.

This theme reappeared in Turner's second blessing, the "general destruction of slavery." For Turner, slavery was a "reactionary cause" that "rebounded back upon the white man, while at the same time "it degraded the status of the black."

> This trafficking in human blood, buying and selling, separating man and wife, parents and children; hardening the hearts and numbed the conscience of the whites and made them cruel and wicked. It petrified their sympathies and deadens their fine sense of justice, and made their moral ideas a blank scroll. The result was, they were not near so benevolent in charitable acts as they should have been; consequently, thousands of white children grew up in their midst without any education for the want of free schools. On the other hand, it tended to make us thievish because we regarded it right to filch what we should have had as the reward for our labor. It also tended to make us untruthful, telling lies to escape punishment or to deceive our owners for some personal comfort which our best men would regard as a necessary perquisite. (*Celebration* 12)

Turner argued that a reactionary curse not only damaged blacks but it also damaged whites as well. This was a long-standing argument that many abolitionists used in support of the eradication of slavery. However, Turner's analysis went deeper. For Turner slavery "numbed the conscience of whites" and caused them to be "cruel and wicked." Turner reasoned that whites have a "fine sense of justice" but that sense of justice was "deadened" and morals turned into a black scroll during slavery. The institution of slavery was so powerful that whites could not be kind and considerate to anybody—even their own children grew up "without any education" because of the want of "free schools."

Of course, the institution of slavery in many ways affected blacks, but here Turner speaks about the spiritual effects. For Turner, enslaved people stole and lied because of slavery; they stole because they thought they had earned whatever they stole and they lied because they wanted "personal comfort," something that anyone would consider a "perquisite." By referring to the circumstances of slavery, Turner attempted to soften his critique while not dismissing it totally. He wanted his audience to know that while he believed that stealing and lying are both morally wrong, one must examine the conditions and situations that place people in those circumstances. For Turner, in slavery, neither blacks nor whites lived as truly free people because of the institution. Slavery trapped whites into being people who took out much of their frustration on themselves, and slavery kept blacks from living authentic and truth-telling lives.

The next "gratitude" comes in the way of "freedoms" that Turner addressed to the blacks in the audience. The first one was the "freedom of schools." While Turner celebrated the reading of all books, he gives special attention to the Bible. "The Bible," Turner proclaimed, "God's eternal will and requirements, was a sealed book. His pledge, his sacred truths, and all the guarantees of his grace were barred and halted against us by the law of the land." Here Turner alluded to the Bible being a "sealed book" for the enslaved because they were forbidden to read, and for Turner that meant that enslaved people were not privy to knowing the "sacred truths," and the "guarantees" of God's grace.

Turner's mention of enslaved people not being able, or owners not allowing them, to read the Bible coincides with his "freedom of the gospel" later in the speech.

> This is a day of gratitude for the freedom of the gospel. Formerly the Southern ministers were chained or curbed in proclaiming the mandates of Heaven. If one felt disposed to preach the whole meaning of the text "to do unto all men as you would have them do unto you," he trembled, feared, and flagged. The learned men of the world were shut out from the South. You could not preach the pure gospel or anyone else. God's word had to be frittered, smeared, and smattered to please the politics of slavery. (*Celebration* 13)

For Turner, whites not only forbade slaves to read the Gospel, but their hearing of the Gospel was "chained and curbed" as well. Not only the enslaved however, but also whites, heard a limited Gospel. Not allowed to hear the meaning of a whole text, some of the major pronouncements—for example, Jesus' mandate "do unto others as you have them do unto you"—did not get a full exposition. In other words, preachers had to play to the politics of slavery in order to proclaim the Gospel, which by Turner's estimation was not a "pure gospel at all." Therefore, for the enslaved, this became tragic because not only were they not hearing a pure Gospel, they also could not read the Gospel for themselves. Whites, on the other hand, were just as hamstrung because even though preachers wanted to preach the whole meaning of the text, they did not do so because of the institution of slavery.

After naming more "freedoms" that blacks can enjoy, Turner turned his attention back to the covenant. In short, he asked blacks in the audience to celebrate the covenant.

> The nation's great emblem is no longer against us for we can claim the protection of the Stars and Stripes. The glories of its fadeless escutcheon will ever bid us go free. Its mighty forts, guns, and magazines have Liberty engraved upon their thundering music. The constitution has covenanted with us for mutual protection: it says: "save me should a foul hand attempt to desecrate my folds, and I will save you from the iron hell of oppression." (*Celebration* 13)

The reason for celebration was that blacks were now part of the covenant and enjoyed the protection of the covenant's military might and the Constitution. Turner further states that the "superstructor [sic] known as Might" was struck down first on January 1, 1863 "by the thunderbolt of emancipation," the "Juno hands of Abraham Lincoln." At first glance, one may read this and perhaps think that Turner was mistaken with his Roman gods. One could argue that Turner meant to say "Jupiter" who was the chief god in Roman mythology. Juno was his wife and sister.

However, an understanding of what "Jupiter" represented maybe would help explain Turner's reference. "Jupiter" was chief among all gods and protector of the Roman government. If "Jupiter" was what Turner meant, he saw Lincoln as a protector of the government and as protector, he had to declare emancipation because slavery did not live up to the covenant relationship that America had with God to be the "proclaimer [sic] of liberty throughout the land."

Turner's Prophetic Encouragement and Hope

Throughout his speech, Turner grounds himself in the sacred, offers a narrative of real situations, and critiques and charges, but he also grounds himself in hope. Turner's hope sprang from the belief that America had a divine mission to promote freedom and equality throughout the world. He believed that now since slavery, that "horrid monster and curse" is dead, America could live up to its promise of equality. It was with this belief that Turner can provide a three-fold basis for hope.

First, Turner believed that whites and blacks could eventually "live in friendship," but, this belief was conditional: "I must say, as I believe, that as soon as old things can be forgotten, *or* all things common, that the Southern people (whites) will take us by the hand and welcome us to their respect and regard" (*Celebration* 13). The key word was "or." The possibility of blacks and whites coming together depended on either forgetting the past or making "all things common."

This functioned rhetorically because Turner did not want to forget the past. He had spent the majority of the speech recalling the past and past events. Remembering the past was of paramount importance. In fact, Turner insists on recounting the horrors of slavery not because he wanted to "incite passions" against white people, but to demonstrate reasons why blacks should "thank God" and "hold this day in special remembrance" (*Celebration* 14). In other words, Turner believed that his slavery narrative was reason to celebrate God's goodness and God's Providence was evident in the destruction of slavery. Therefore, out of this Providence, Turner's hope was for equality between blacks and whites and the only way for this to occur is for all things to be common.

Turner's hope also leads him to offer a challenge and charge to blacks in his audience:

> Let us love the whites, and let by-gones be by-gones, neither taunt nor insult them for past grievances, respect them; honor them; work for them; but still let us be men. Let us show them we can be a people, respectable, virtuous, honest, and industrious, and soon their prejudice will melt away, and with God for our father, we will all be brothers. (*Celebration* 14)

Turner's charge to blacks was to "love the whites" and "let by-gones be by-gones." Turner did not want blacks to forget about slavery because forgetting about slavery and its horrors would deny Providence. Instead, Turner challenged blacks not to hold slavery against whites and to respect, honor, and work for whites without sacrificing their personhood. Turner believed that white "prejudice will melt away" because with God as Father both blacks and whites could be brothers. Turner believed in the unity of humanity and America as the bastion of liberty and freedom for both blacks and whites.

By all accounts, Turner's speech was a success and despite the rainy weather and the fact that the "streets and roads were almost impassable," almost 3,000 people showed up for the "first anniversary of freedom." The crowd was thoroughly impressed with Turner and according to Robert Kent, Chairman of the event, the crowd was "amused and astonished" at the "lofty language and eloquence" of Turner (27 Jan. 1866). He further wrote, "Even the whites could not conceal their admiration, nor restrain the applause due him, as the best orator of the day."

Given, as the pamphlet noted, on "the spur of the moment," Turner attempted to place the new day of "emancipation" (January 1), within the context of other days celebrated by Americans. This new day or new era could only come about in Turner's estimation because America was divinely inspired. For Turner, America was the "stone cut from the mountain"—fulfilling biblical prophecy as a messianic nation called by God to promote liberty and freedom for the oppressed. Although slavery (in the form that it took) was a stain on the country and a sin, it was Turner's belief in the American creed that allowed him to offer a reinterpretation of slavery. For Turner slavery, while wrong in the sight of God (he would later call slavery a providential institution and not a divine one), did not displace America from its chosen position. America needed to be judged for its sins, and for Turner, God's judgment took the form of the Civil War. It was through the Civil War and the Union's victory that God answered the prayers of millions of blacks and finally destroyed slavery. Therefore, for Turner, with slavery abolished, America could finally live up to the covenant and be a place of liberty for both blacks and whites.

Turner's belief and hope in the covenant and in America culminated in his *eight blessings or freedoms* that ends the speech. By promoting these blessings and freedoms, Turner positioned himself as a covenantal prophet for both blacks and whites because he saw these blessings and freedoms intertwining to produce the foundation of mutuality Turner felt important to the future of the South. It is only by working together and respecting one another that prejudice will "melt away" and Turner's vision of unity and of brother and sisterhood will become a reality.

It was with this optimistic tone that Turner began his work in the South. Grounded in the belief that "by-gones should be by-gones," and along with the belief that blacks and whites could work together in the South, Turner involved himself in a host of activities. He not only established the AME Church in Georgia, but also involved himself in politics, helping establish Loyalty Leagues and writing pamphlets for the Republican Party.

However, Turner did not stay optimistic for long, and his belief in the American covenant was about to be put to a test and shook to its core. In an impassioned speech delivered from the floor of the Georgia House, Turner offered a prophetic rebuke of his opponents as he defended the right of blacks to serve in the legislature. This speech began Turner's prophetic shift that would grow more pessimistic as America defaulted on its promise to African Americans.

Notes

1. Turner would also become a big proponent of education. To read more about Turner's advocacy for education during the Civil War see Andrea Heather Williams' *Self-Taught: African American Education in Slavery and Freedom*, especially chapter 3.

2. For more on Emancipation Day celebrations see Mitch Kachun's *Festival of Freedom: Memory and Meaning in African American Emancipation Celebrations, 1808-1915*.

3. For more on August 1st celebrations, see Detine Bowers, "A Place to Stand: African Americans and the First of August Platform," *Southern Communication Journal* 60.4 (1995): 348-361.

4. After Emancipation and the ratification of the Thirteenth Amendment, January 1 becomes the date of many Emancipation Day celebrations in the South. See chapter three of Mitch Kachun's *Festivals of Freedom: Memory and Meaning in African American Emancipation Celebrations*.

5. For a further explanation of the chosen nation myth, see Richard Hughes, *Myths America Lives By* (Champaign: Univ. of Illinois Press, 2003).

6. Turner's interpretation was not new. This belief had been a strain in African American oratory for decades. See Peter Williams' speech "Abolition of the Slave Trade" in *Lift Every Voice: African American Oratory 1787-1900*, ed. Philip Foner and Robert James Branham (Tuscaloosa: Univ. of Alabama Press, 1998).

7. Many have used the Curse of Noah, found in chapter nine of the biblical book of Genesis, as justification to enslave Africans. The teaching held that Noah cursed Canaan to be servants and "hewers of wood" to his brothers forever. It held that "Africans" were descendents of Canaan and therefore the ones suited for slavery. I discuss this teaching in detail in chapter three.

Chapter Two

"Hurling Thunderbolts" and "Fighting the Devil with Fire": Turner's Prophetic Disputation

In 1866, Turner devoted much of his time to the building of the AME Church in Georgia. However, he still found time for politics. Just ten days after his well-received Emancipation Day speech, Turner participated in the Freedmen's Convention in Augusta, Georgia. Delegates called the statewide convention to discuss and "take into consideration their new positions to society as freemen and the duties upon them" (*Freemen's Convention* Jan. 20, 1866). Despite the short notice of the Convention and the "uncertainty of communication," the Convention by all accounts was a success. However, instead of a radical agenda, the Convention only proposed modest plans. While many believed that the Convention would propose "nothing short of immediate suffrage and seats in the present legislature," one writer observing the proceedings remarked that to the contrary, "their whole deliberations are characterized with an extreme want of extravagance and arrogance" (*Freedmen's Convention*).

Indeed, the majority of the proposals in the Freedmen's Convention were quite modest. The Convention opposed universal suffrage and advocated that the state only allow blacks who could read or write and who possessed "certain proper qualifications" the right of suffrage. While members of the Convention did form the Equal Rights Association of Georgia, the purpose of the Association was to promote "principles of honesty, industry, and sobriety." Further, they were to "persuade their brethren to entertain kind feelings to their former masters and to faithful observe contracts." They were to learn that it would be only by "hard work and integrity" that they would ever hope to gain respect and further they were to put away any notion that they were to gain possession of any land without paying the rightful owner (*Colored Convention* Jan. 30, 1866).

It was in the spirit of moderation that Turner began his political work in the South. Fueled by the Reconstruction measures passed in March of 1867, the Republican Party hired Turner as a spokesperson and Turner thrived in the position. He wrote a highly successful pamphlet that promoted reasons why the Republican Party was the better party for African Americans. He urged blacks to join the Union Leagues and to organize in associations that would benefit African Americans politically

Concerning race issues, Turner continued his moderate tone in a speech given in Columbia, South Carolina in April 1867. Turner reminded his audience composed of blacks and whites that, "the difference of race is nothing, therefore the interests of white and black are one and the same—all are citizens in common. It therefore behooves both colors to cooperate, to join hands and to strive to the same goal ("Affairs," *NYT* 1). Further, he declared that he wanted to see a "united south" and "notwithstanding the education of the past," he believed that "the Southern gentlemen were the best and truest friend of the Negro" ("Political" Apr. 30, 1867). By August of that year, however, and despite Turner's pleas for unity, he noticed both sides of the Reconstruction debate heating up. "Politically things are hot, at boiling point," he wrote, but he felt that the state would eventually pass the Reconstruction Measures ("Rev. H M Turner" Aug. 17, 1867).

While taking a week-long vacation in Indian Springs, Arkansas during the month of August, Turner contemplated an early retirement. In a letter to the *Christian Recorder* Turner reflected on his life, as he desired to spend more time with his family.

> I have been away from my family for so long, roaming over the hills and through the valleys of this country; first in search of the freedom of my race, then the social, moral and intellectual elevation, that my four little children at home, whom I have not seen more than once a year, can barely recognize me, much less know a father's love or feel a father's wrath. . . . I hope to retire in peace to the comfortable shades of my family circle and to the more limited responsibilities of the pastoral work. ("Letter from Rev H M Turner," Aug. 31, 1867)

However, Turner had to place contemplation and talk about retirement and spending more time with family on hold. One part of the Reconstruction Act of 1867 was that all the succeeding states must hold a convention to draft a new constitution for admittance back into the Union. Georgia held a three-day election to elect representatives to the state convention from October 29 to November 2, 1867. With most to the Democrats and other conservative whites not participating in the convention election, Republicans made up the majority of delegates when the Constitutional Convention met in December. However, contrary to the majority of reports at the time, the majority of the delegates were moderate and not radical and while there were cries of "Negro Rule" during this time, of the 169 delegates only thirty-seven were African American (Herndon 16).

Turner was one of the thirty-seven and immediately presented a reserved and conciliatory tone in the proceedings. According to one historian, Turner's "conduct throughout the course of the convention reflected a sincere desire to cooperate with the white community in formulating a sound and workable constitution for the state" (Herndon 18). Another one noted that Turner's demeanor while "strategic in character," was nevertheless "quite conservative, almost to a fault (Angell 85). Moreover, an examination of Turner's actions while a delegate to the Constitutional Convention would tend to support Herndon's claims that Turner demonstrated a "naive faith" in the white citizens of Georgia. For instance, Turner favored protecting property rights of the Confederate upper class, while also removing suffrage restrictions against them. This allowed former Confederates in 1868 to win election to the state legislature. He favored pardoning Jefferson Davis and proposed an educational amendment for voting. He also favored what many would later call a poll tax that conservatives used to disenfranchise African Americans (Herndon 18-21, Angell 85-86).

However, according to Herndon, the biggest example of Turner's naiveté was "his failure to foresee the implications of the omission from the Georgia Constitution of an explicit provision" that guaranteed African Americans the right to hold public office (21). Members of his own party convinced Turner that the state constitution did not need this provision in order to protect African American rights. So Turner did not vote for the provision—a mistake that Turner would later regret.

Due to the hard work and conciliatory nature that Turner and other black delegates fostered during the Constitutional Convention in June 1868, the people of Georgia (Bibb County) elected Henry McNeal Turner and twenty-four other African Americans to the Georgia House of Representatives. However, August 8 of that same year, a resolution was introduced that would deny all African American members the right to serve in the legislature (Martin 48). Led by conservatives in both parties, the advocates for expulsion argued that African Americans could not hold office primarily for three reasons: African Americans had not contributed anything to history; Congress never gave African Americans the right to hold office, and there had not been a specific enactment conferred upon African Americans to hold office. Other arguments for expulsion included that because African Americans were once slaves and therefore not properly educated, they did not have the necessary acumen to deliberate on political matters and the belief that African Americans had never built any monuments. However, the most frequently articulated argument against African Americans holding office was of course, the one Turner voted against, that the United States or the Georgia state constitution had not granted the rights of African Americans to hold elected office.

After much debate on the measure to expel African American members of the House, Turner addressed the body on September 3, 1868. Commonly called *"I Claim the Rights of a Man,"* this speech has been anthologized, albeit in edited versions, in three major works: in Redkey's *Respect Black: Writings and Speeches of Henry McNeal Turner*, in Foner's *Lift Every Voice: African American Oratory 1787-1900*, and more recently in Howard Zinn's and Anthony Arnove's *Voices of a People's History of the United States*. In addition, one can find excerpts of the speech widely distributed over the Internet.

Scholars have called this speech one of Turner's finest. Herndon called the speech "both an impassioned statement of the Negro's rights and a lucid assertion of the illegality of the legislature's action" (25). Dittmer called the speech the "most powerful of his [Turner's] career" and a "manifesto for human rights" (258). Angell simply called the speech "powerful" (Angell, *Bishop* 88).

The speech consisted of an introduction in which Turner establishes his "position" followed by a series of rhetorical questions aimed at securing this position. Second, Turner turned his attention to disputing and refuting his opponent's claims, which makes up the majority of his speech, and finally, Turner offers a prophetic warning that House members will have to answer to God for the actions that they take.

On the Eligibility of Colored Members to Seats in the Georgia Legislature

Introduction

Turner wastes no time establishing the tone and tenor of the speech:

> Before proceeding to argue this question upon its intrinsic merits, I wish the Members of this House to understand the position that I take. I hold that I am a member of this body. Therefore, sir, I shall neither fawn nor cringe before any party, nor stoop to beg them for my rights. Some of my colored fellow-members, in the course of their remarks, took occasion to appeal to the *sympathies* of Members on the opposite side, and to eulogize their character for magnanimity. It reminds me very much, sir, of slaves begging under the lash. I am here to demand my rights, and to hurl thunderbolts at men who would dare to cross the threshold of my manhood. There is an old aphorism which says, "Fight the Devil with fire," and if I should observe the rule in this instance, I wish gentlemen to understand that it is but fighting them with their own weapon. (Turner, *Eligibility* 82)

Turner immediately adopts a prophetic persona by establishing the position that he takes in the speech. Turner's "position" will not allow him to "fawn," "cringe," or "stoop" for his rights. Turner's *position* is to "demand his rights" and to "hurl thunderbolts" at anyone who "would dare to cross the threshold of my manhood." He takes this strong "position" because he grounds himself in the belief that he is a "member of this body" and as a member, he has the right to speak and defend himself against the charges that he would later address.

By grounding himself as a member of the House and standing in the "position" to demand his rights as a member, Turner becomes a *voice crying in the wilderness*—one who stands *with and against* his audience both at the same time. His position as lone prophet gains strength because he does not appeal to the *sympathies* of his enemies or "eulogize their character for magnanimity" as other black members did. For Turner, these "enemies" lost all the respect they once had, and he refuses to appeal to them because to do so would be to return to the days of slavery when slaves begged "under the lash." Therefore Turner believes the best way to handle this injustice is to "fight the Devil with fire" because he believes that his enemies are fighting with fire, and the only response is found in the old adage "fight fire with fire."

By establishing this position, Turner rhetorically frames his argument as a fight against the Devil. In this way, Turner can prophetically stand with God, stand against his opponents and stand up for the other African American members who in Turner's estimation needed someone to stand and speak for them. Turner felt that the members were returning to slavery by appealing to their opponents' sympathies and eulogizing their "character[s] for magnanimity." Turner's belief in his opponent's "sympathy" and "magnanimity" disappears when his opponents introduces the motion to expel the African American legislators.

This realization for Turner also helps to strengthen his prophetic persona— Turner does not have to worry about consensus building or being a prophet for everyone (entire audience). Here he represents the feelings and emotions of the African American members of the house. To buttress this claim, later in the speech when Turner proclaims that he is speaking for himself while black members of the House may not endorse his sentiments, they all cried out "we do" (86), thus allowing Turner to become the leader of the African American representatives and to strengthen his prophetic persona.

Further, for Turner, the expelling of the African American members of the House grounded itself in the belief that African Americans were not human. Positioned this way, Turner can later ask, "Am I a man—If I am such, I claim the rights of a man" (83). Foreshadowing the Memphis sanitation workers' struggle for just and humane treatment from the city when they declared, "I am a man," Turner prophetically aimed at what he believed was the most significant part of his opponent's arguments. For Turner, it was simple: if one believed that he and his fellow African American members were human, then they could serve; if they were deemed not human, then they could not serve in the House or take any part of elective office. When Turner claimed the "rights of a man," he included in those rights the right to participate in the political process. Turner believed he was "entitled" to his seat in the House and was ready to argue the question "upon its intrinsic merits."

How did Turner argue this question "upon its intrinsic merits"? I maintain that Turner grounded himself in prophetic discourse that allowed him to not only critique his opponents but also establish himself not only as a spokesperson/prophet for African Americans representatives that day, but also for the entire African American community.

Turner's Sacred Grounding

To answer the question, "Am I a man?" Turner offers a two-fold answer. First, he grounds his answer in the *sacred character of God.*

> God saw fit to vary everything in Nature. There are no two men alike—no two voices alike—no two trees alike. God has weaved and tissued variety and versatility throughout the boundless space of creation. Because God saw fit to make some red, and some white, and some black, and some brown, are we to sit in judgment upon what God has seen fit to do? As well might one play with the thunderbolts of heaven as with that creature that bears God's image—God's photograph (84).

By grounding his argument in the *sacred character* of God, not only did Turner highlight the diversity of God, who has "weaved and tissued variety and versatility throughout the boundless space of creation," he also attacked the position of his opponents. Since his opponents attempted to expel African American members from the House as a result of their racist beliefs, Turner framed and grounded his answer in the sacred character of God. Framed this way, Turner placed the onus of the "color problem" not on African Americans, but on God. "Because God saw fit" to do this, Turner then can ask the rhetorical question "are we to sit in judgment upon what God has seen fit to do"?

Here Turner invited his opponents to reflect on the events taking place in the House. By expelling the African American members of the House, Turner's opponents in essence rejected a part of the *character and nature of God.* Moreover, not only did they reject the character and nature of God, but also by expelling the African American members, Turner's opponents rejected God's "image and photograph." Grounded in the concept of the *sacred character and nature of God,* Turner was able to extend this concept when he declared, "I do not regard this movement as a thrust at me. It is a thrust at the bible—a thrust at the God of the Universe, for making a man and not finishing him; it is simply calling the Great Jehovah a fool" (93).

Turner's opponents' attack was not against him (or the other African American members of the House), but an attack against the Bible and against God. When he shifted his opponents' attacks to God, Turner implied that blame did not lie at the feet of the African American representatives, but assigned blame to God for "making some white and some black." However, to blame or make an attack such as this one on God was to open oneself to the charge of blasphemy. To say and believe this was to challenge the sacred character of God because of the theological position that God does not make mistakes. When framed this way, Turner not only took the moral high ground in the debate to dispute and refute his opponents, but he also expressed his *radical belief* of the inclusiveness of God.

While Turner's rhetorical strategy invited his audience (made up primarily of his opponents) to reflect on their actions and to a larger degree, to reflect on their view of God and the Bible, Turner also articulated an *empowerment theology* directed toward African Americans. Within this theology, what Turner proclaimed to African Americans is that God made them the way they are, but more importantly, *there was nothing wrong in being black*. For Turner, God was a God of diversity. God decided the make-up of a person and while God made all differently, God make all in the image of God's self.

The power of this message must not be underestimated because the theology of the day maintained a different attitude toward African Americans. Many people believed God did not create African Americans *in God's image* or in the same way God created whites, or that, at best, God created African Americans inherently inferior to whites. Many Southern pastors and ministers believed and preached this brand of Christianity to their congregations because they argued that God had ordained and ordered the races in a hierarchal structure—with whites on top and blacks near or at the bottom.[1] Turner attempted to reverse this line of thinking.

The second way that Turner answers the question of "Am I a man" is by grounding himself in the sacredness of the United States Constitution. Turner states:

> In the course of this discussion, a good deal of reference has been made to the Constitution; *I am as much a man as anybody else*. I hold that that document is neither proscripted, or has it ever, in the first instance, sanctioned slavery (87).

The Constitution as America's *sacred document*, along with the Declaration of Independence, has always been a part of the American Creed. Both have acted as a covenantal agreement that binds Americans as one. However, instead of calling his audience to live up to the sacred principles found in the Constitution, Turner invoked the document here to prove that he too is a *man* protected by the Constitution's sacred principles. Therefore, Turner grounded himself in this covenant and proclaimed that the Constitution declared that he was as "much a man as anybody else" (87).

But for Turner, how did the Constitution make him a man? It made him a man because the Constitution never sanctioned slavery. Recalling Turner's Emancipation Day speech, there was a clear line of demarcation between being a slave and being free. For Turner, to be a slave meant that one was not a citizen, but to be free amounted to being a citizen and enjoying the rights and privileges thereof. Thus, Turner juxtaposes slavery and personhood. To be a slave is not to be a person but to be free is to be a person and free persons have rights assigned to them.

Therefore, for Turner, the Constitution did not endorse or sanction slavery because it was part of the American Creed along with the Declaration that
declared "all men equal" and second, if the Constitution endorsed slavery; then
it could not make him or other African Americans citizens or persons. So he,
like Fredrick Douglass before him,[2] argued for a reinterpretation of the *sacred
document*. Turner started his defense of the Constitution by arguing against what
he believed was a false interpretation.

> The Constitution says that any person escaping from service in one state, and
> going to another, shall on demand, be given up. That has been the clause under
> which the democratic fire-eaters have maintained that that document sanctioned
> slavery in man. I shall show you that it meant no such thing. It was placed
> there, according to Mr. Madison, altogether for a different purpose . . . Mr.
> Madison declared, he "thought it wrong to admit in the Constitution the idea
> that there could be property of man." . . . The word "SERVITUDE" was struck
> out, and "service" unanimously inserted—the former being thought to express
> the conditions of SLAVES, and the latter the obligation of free person. (87,
> emphasis in the original)

Turner's opponents argued that slavery was lawful because the Constitution
"sanctioned slavery in man." Turner countered this argument by offering a reinterpretation of the Constitution. By invoking the Founding Fathers' position on
slavery, Turner rhetorically restructured the argument and debate about the Constitution.

First, for Turner, while the Constitution provided that any person escaping
from service in one state and going to another, "shall on demand be given up," it
could not have referred to slavery. Turner highlighted the Founders intent and
provided the audience with a *history lesson* of sorts as he explained that the
Founders took out the word "SERVITUDE" and replaced it with "service." For
Turner, this was a *conscious choice* because the Founders did not want to be
misinterpreted. Turner's argument was simple; if the Founders wanted slavery,
they would have used that word in the Constitution. Since it was not there, he
concluded that they never wanted the country to be a slave-holding nation.

Therefore, by adopting the "neutral position" argument about the Constitution and its relation to slavery, Turner embraced the fullness of the document
and held it up as *sacred text*. By engaging the text this way, Turner grounded his
speech within this covenant which leads him to later declare, "Every law, therefore, which is passed under the Constitution of the United States, is a portion of
the Supreme Law of the Land, and you are bound to obey it" (87). Moreover,
framed this way, Turner placed the Georgia House on notice. Any law or any
bill must pass Constitutional muster, because Georgia law was under the U.S.
Constitution and the U.S. Constitution was the "supreme law of the land," and
he and his opponents were "bound to obey it."

However, Congress amended the Constitution since the days of the Founders. Therefore, Turner used this to bolster his claim of being a person and citi-

zen. After quoting the newly ratified Fourteenth Amendment, Turner proclaimed:

> For what purpose was this clause inserted in that Constitution? It was placed there, sir, to protect the rights of every man—the heaven-granted, inalienable, unrestricted rights of mine, and of my race. Great God, if I had the voice of seven thunders, today, I would make the ends of the earth to hear me. (90)

Turner strengthened his reinterpretation of the Constitution. Even if one believed prior to the ratification of the Fourteenth Amendment that African Americans were not citizens (Dred Scott case), Turner wanted to make clear that all citizens'—including African Americans'—rights are protected. However, these were not just any rights—they were "heaven-granted," "inalienable," "unrestricted rights"—in short, *sacred rights*. Turner made clear that these "rights" are primarily from God and now since these rights are part of the sacred document of America, they belong not only in the spiritual but temporal realms as well.[3]

Prophetic Refutations

The second and longest part of Turner's speech was his use of refutations. Turner's first disputation and refutation comes when he addresses the question, "What has the Negro race done?"

> Well Mr. Speaker, all I have to say upon the subject is this: that if we are the class of people that we are generally represented to be, I hold that we are a great people. It is generally considered that we are the children of Canaan and the curse of the father rest upon our heads, and has rested, all through history. Sir I deny that the curse of Noah has anything to do with the Negro. We are not the children of Canaan. . . . We are the children of Cush, and Canaan's curse has nothing whatever to do with the Negro. If we belong to that race, Ham belonged to it, under whose instructions Napoleon Bonaparte studied military tactics. If we belong to that race, St. Augustine belonged to it. (84)

Turner did not directly answer the question, but he opted to address the so-called *"curse of Noah"* or *curse of Canaan theory*. Turner chose this strategy to address the prevailing ideology and theology of the day before he addressed the question directly. Since his opponents used the curse of Noah to justify the enslavement of blacks and to *prove* black inferiority, Turner decided to discredit the theory before he addressed the question. He would have known that behind the question lay the belief in black inferiority.

Turner elected to address the "theory" by simply denying any "negro" association with the curse. The curse of Noah did not have "anything to do with the Negro" because blacks are "children of Cush." It is interesting here that Turner did not disavow the curse or claim that the curse was wrong; for Turner, people who used it to prove black inferiority have just misapplied the curse.

Once Turner established blacks as descendents of Cush instead of the *cursed people* of Canaan, he directly answered the question. If Turner was correct in his assumptions, Ham belonged to the black race. The intent was to demonstrate that blacks, in the line of Cush, had major accomplishments.

Turner participated in what Wilson Moses calls *vindicationism*. The term *vindicationist*, to quote Moses, "refers to a unique tradition among people of African ancestry, the project of defending black people from the charge that they have made little or no contribution to the history of human progress" (Moses, *Afrotopia* 21). Many African American orators and writers in the nineteenth century grounded themselves within this tradition to prove their worthiness. Within this tradition, many African Americans found great tools of invention, both sacred and secular, that refuted charges that blacks had not contributed to the history of the world.

However, Turner abruptly shifted from his previous line of thought and turned to his major issue: "The negro is here charged with holding office." To refute this charge, Turner developed a three-fold argument that takes up the majority of his speech. Turner argued that the "negro never wanted office," and when candidates were needed for the constitutional convention, blacks went "door to door in the 'negro belt' and begged white men to run" (85). In fact, according to Turner's refutation of the charge, white men "induced the colored man to place his name upon the ticket as a candidate for the Convention." All the black people wanted to do according to Turner was to be able to "walk up to the polls and deposit our ballots" (85).

The reason why whites wanted blacks to run was that one of the white leaders, Benjamin Hill, told them that it was a "nigger affair" and advised whites to stay away from the polls. By recalling this bit of history, Turner proclaimed:

> If the "niggers" had "office on the brain," it was the white man that put it there—not carpet-baggers, either, nor Yankees, nor scalawags, but high bred and dignified democracy of the South. And if anyone is to blame for having Negroes in these legislative halls—if blame attaches to it at all—it is the Democratic Party. Now however, a change has come over the spirit of their dream. They want to turn the "nigger" out; and, to support their argument, they say that the black man is debarred from holding office by the Reconstruction measures of Congress. (85)

His critique of the Democrats was reminiscent of his critique of whites for slavery in his *Emancipation Day* speech; he placed the blame on his opponents. In other words, for Turner, the reason why blacks went to the polls and voted for a Constitutional Convention that eventually led to blacks being elected was that whites not only did not participate in the voting process, but *whites encouraged blacks to run and serve*. For Turner, this was the height of hypocrisy—Democrats argued that African Americans are not entitled by the Reconstruction measures to hold the very offices that they were encouraged to seek.

The second part of his argument to the charge of "negroes holding office" was to refute the belief that *Congress never gave the right to African Americans to hold office.* Turner argued that Congress based the Reconstruction measures "on the ground that no distinction should be made on account of race, color, or previous condition" and therefore they permitted blacks to hold office. Speaking further on the Reconstruction measures Turner stated:

> Was not that the grand fulcrum on which they rested? And did not every reconstructed state have to reconstruct on the idea that no discrimination, in any sense of the term, should be made? There is not a man here who would dare say "no." If Congress has simply given me merely sufficient civil and political rights to make me a mere political slave for Democrats, or anybody else— giving then the opportunity of jumping on my back, in order to leap into political power—I do not thank Congress for it. Never, so help me God, shall I be a political slave. (86)

Opponents also had argued that neither the Fourteenth Amendment nor Georgia's current state constitution provided a place for African Americans to hold office. However, here Turner did not appeal to either of these documents individually but to the "Reconstruction measures" in their entirety.[4] When he used the term "Reconstruction measures" Turner did not want to limit the debate to any particular law or measure—he wanted to address the spirit of the measures. For Turner, the Reconstruction measures provided a space for nondiscriminatory practices and any "reconstructed" state had to accept the spirit of the measure, or in Turner words, "reconstruct on the idea that no discrimination for any reason should be made." In other words, the former Confederate states had to turn from their position of discrimination to a newly constructed idea of racial equality.

Confident in his hermeneutical approach on this subject, he later challenged any of his opponents to "submit to Congress for an explanation as to *what was meant* in the passage of their Reconstruction measures or the Georgia convention that framed the Constitution under which we are acting" (86-87). It was Turner's belief that either body would support his assertion that the Reconstruction measures promoted a nondiscriminatory policy.

Turner's appeal to the spirit of the law functioned rhetorically because it took the focus off the narrow, legalistic interpretation of any *one law* and placed the interpretive lens on the measures (laws) as a whole. What Turner did was to focus on the intent of the measures: what Congress and the state of Georgia intended to do when they passed these laws. Turner drew upon the intent of the "Reconstruction measures" and argued that the framers of the measure intended to eradicate all discrimination—in "any sense of the term"—based on the doctrine of universal human rights. Thus, Turner grounded himself in the sacredness of the Constitution as well as God who is the dispenser of these universal human rights.

Turner further argued that refusing to allow African Americans to hold office was not only to stand against the Constitution and God, but it was also tantamount to placing African Americans back into a type of slavery. Turner maintained that it is "political slavery" for a group of people to have "civil and political rights" but not to allow them to hold office. Turner saw this as an attack on his personhood that would allow others (whites) to assume political power on the backs of blacks. He declared later with other black representatives cheering him on, "But assisting Mr. Lincoln to take me out of servile slavery, did not intend to put me and my race into political slavery. If they did, let them take away my ballot—I do not want it and shall not have it" (86).

The third part of Turner's refutation referred to the claim that African Americans could not hold office because holding elective office was not "conferred" upon blacks by "specific enactment." To answer this objection, Turner posed a rhetorical question; "Were we ever made slaves by specific enactment?" Then he added:

> I hold sir, that there never was a law passed in this country, from its foundation to the Emancipation, which enacted us as slaves. . . . If, then, you have no laws enacting me a slave, how can you question my right to my freedom? . . . Why then do gentlemen clamor for proof of our being free "by virtue of specific enactment?" Show me any specific law of Georgia, or of the United States, that enacted black men to be slaves, and I will tell you that, before we can enjoy our rights as free men, such law must be repealed. (89)

Turner drew upon the use of rhetorical questions to counter the argument that passage of a specific enactment was necessary before blacks could hold office. However, Turner addressed more in this passage. He equated the right to hold office with the right of *freedom*. Recalling Turner's Emancipation speech, there are only two positions one can hold in America—slave or free. For Turner, the denial of his "right" to hold office infringed on his right to be free and placed him as he had said earlier, as a "political slave" (86).

The fourth and final refutation against the view that African Americans could not hold office related to the claim that blacks had not built any monuments. This charge, aimed at the intellectual capacity of blacks, grounded itself in the belief that since they had not built any monuments, they did not have the capacity to serve in politics. Turner could have answered the charge in vindicationist terms by invoking the pyramids of Egypt, the civilizations of Africa, or even talk about the many structures and buildings that enslaved Africans erected in the South. However, Turner chose a different approach that challenged his audience:

> I can tell the gentlemen one thing; that is, that we could have built monuments of fire while the war was in progress. We could have fired your woods, your barns and fences and call you home. Did we do it? No sir: and God grant that the Negro may never do it, or do anything else that would destroy the good reputation of his friends. No epithet is sufficiently opprobrious for us now. I

say sir that we have built a monument of docility, of obedience, of respect and of self-control that will endure longer than the Pyramids of Egypt. (95)

Instead of speaking about literal monuments, Turner spoke about symbolic ones. First, Turner spoke about the "monuments of fire" that could have been built during the war. As in his earlier *Emancipation Day* speech, Turner deployed one of the rhetorical strategies blacks used to illicit sympathy from whites, which was to invoke the response of Southern blacks during the war. Many blacks argued that slaves could have run away or destroyed their master's property while they were away fighting in the war, but because of an obedient and docile nature, blacks did not take that course of action. Why did slaves not take this action? Turner answered the question when he explained that blacks did not want to destroy the "good opinion" they had with their friends, and blacks were at work building monuments of docility, obedience, respect, and self-control.

Turner invoked the *docile Negro* myth. While contemporary scholars have debunked the myth of the "docile negro," it is important to understand rhetorically why Turner found this to be an important rhetorical strategy.[5] Cal Logue has written about the rhetorical construction of blacks during Reconstruction. He suggested three ways that whites rhetorically constructed blacks that helped shape pubic opinion about African Americans during this period. The first construction was that blacks were barbaric, the second that they were immoral, and finally that they were not fit for self-government (*Rhetorical Ridicule*).

What Turner did when he drew upon the docile Negro myth was to counter-attack these rhetorical constructions. Turner attempted to demonstrate within the speech that blacks were not the wild, crazy beasts that many thought they were, while at the same time addressing the prevailing belief that blacks were immoral. For Turner, not burning woods, barns, and fences when blacks had the chance to do so, proved that they were respectful and in control of their actions. Finally, the fact that Turner spoke in the House that day as well as all of his work previously for the Republican Party and the Constitutional Convention proved that he, as a black person, could govern. Therefore, Turner's use of the docile Negro myth had profound rhetorical implications as part of his strategy to refute the social prejudices of his day.

However, the docile Negro myth also served another function, especially in the rhetoric of Turner. Since Turner adopted a prophetic persona, the docile Negro myth allowed him to seek out and stand on the moral high ground and to place blacks in the role of *persecuted saints*. When framed this way, Turner could juxtapose the actions of black and whites through a *compare and contrast* strategy. When blacks had an opportunity during the war to oppress whites, they did not; however, when whites now have an opportunity to oppress and persecute blacks by denying them seats in the Legislature, whites followed through with their threats. Therefore, Turner demonstrated that African Americans were not the ones who were barbaric and immoral, but that his white opponents were.

However, unlike others who have used the docile Negro myth to construct weakness, Turner's use of it reclaimed agency and choice for African Americans. Turner's declaration, "We could have built monuments of fire while the war was in process," highlighted choice and freedom. During the war, Turner suggested that blacks really had an opportunity to destroy their enemies without fear of any retribution. That black people *did not choose* this option did not mean, in Turner's estimation, that African Americans were weak, passive, or even afraid, it meant that blacks had choices and they did not choose revenge, but chose self-control. In Turner's estimation, this would "endure longer than the pyramids in Egypt."

In short, by drawing on the docile Negro myth, Turner attempted to refute much of the social knowledge of the day. Turner adopted a prophetic identity, claimed the moral high ground, and proclaimed that blacks were not what many perceived them to be. Arguing in this way, Turner created the platform from which to launch stinging critiques and judgments upon his audience.

Turner's Prophetic Critiques and Judgments

Turner's critiques of his audience and the wider society come early and often throughout the speech and focus primarily on two major opponents. The first opponent is the "Anglo-Saxon race" or white people in general.

> The Anglo-Saxon race, sir, is a most surprising one. No man has ever been more deceived in that race than I have been for the last three weeks. I was not aware that there was in the character of that race so much cowardice, or so much pusillanimity. The treachery which has been exhibited in it by gentlemen belonging to that race has shaken my confidence in it more than anything that has come under my observation from my birth. (82)

Many blacks had internalized the views of nineteenth century orators and writers that the Anglo-Saxons were "lovers of liberty," who had the "spirit of individual enterprise and resourcefulness," and a "capacity for practical and reasonable behavior" (Fredrickson 98). In fact, many African Americans held up Anglo-Saxons and their views as ideal—the height of true civilization. As Turner noted earlier in his speech, many of the other black members of the house appealed to this character construction of whites.

However, Turner did not appeal to this conventional wisdom. Instead, he adopted a prophetic persona that allowed him to view his situation as different from that of other Representatives. Turner spoke from the moral high ground, saw the error of his ways and confessed that he too had bought into Anglo-Saxon thought which led him to admit that he had been "deceived" by the white race and was not aware of the "cowardice and pusillanimity" of their characters. Far from regarding whites as courageous and fair-minded, Turner's "confidence" in the race had been shaken. When he framed his critique this way, he then questioned Anglo-Saxon loyalty to the legislature.

Whose Legislature is this? Is it a white man's Legislature, or a black man's Legislature? . . . Did half the white men of Georgia vote for this Legislature? Did not the great bulk of them fight, with all their strength, the Constitution under which we are acting? And did they not fight against the organization of this legislature? And further sir, did they not vote against it? Yes sir! And there are persons in this Legislature, today, who are ready to spit their poison in my face, while they' themselves opposed, with all their power, the ratification of this Constitution. They question my right to a seat in this body. . . . No analogy can be found for it, except it be the case of a man who should go into my house, take possession of my wife and children and then tell me to walk out. . . . We are told that if black men want to speak, they must speak through white trumpets; if black men want their sentiments expressed, they must be adulterated and sent through white messengers. . . . If this be not done, then the black men have committed an outrage, and their representatives must be denied the right to represent their constituents. (83)

Arguing in this way, Turner not only challenged the rhetorical construction of Anglo-Saxonism, he also invited his audience to see the hypocrisy of his opponent's actions. Turner highlighted this hypocrisy when he recalled that white men, and especially white men currently in the Legislature, did not vote for the current makeup of the Legislature in the first place. Indeed, many of them fought against having a Legislature at all, fought against the adoption of the Georgia Constitution, and voted against both.

Moreover, this allowed Turner to reason by answering the rhetorical question: "Whose Legislature is this?" In Turner's estimation, it was a *black man's* Legislature. Since whites did not want anything to do with the creation of the Legislature and in fact did everything in their power to stop it, Turner reasoned that this is a black man's Legislature—and since it is a black man's Legislature and created by the work and votes primarily of black men, then they should serve.

While Turner did not advocate that only African Americans should serve in the House, his strategy here was to *remind his opponents* that African Americans created the Legislature, and since it is their creation, they may serve. Turner makes this point clear when he proclaims:

If I am not permitted to occupy a seat here, for the purpose of representing my constituents, I want to know how white men can be permitted to do so. How can a white man represent a colored constituency, if a colored man cannot do it? . . . Now I want gentlemen to come down to cool common sense. Is the created greater than the Creator? Is man greater than God? It is very strange, if a white man can occupy on this floor a seat *created by colored votes*, and a black man cannot do it. (86, emphasis original)

Turner's arguments foreshadowed political arguments developed later in the twentieth century. Grounded in *representation and agency*, Turner's political theory was clear—a white person should not represent an African American if an African American could not represent that same constituency. The word *"created"* took on a double meaning—first as creation of the Legislature, and second, as the creation of the *position or title of representative* by African American votes. Turner wanted to demonstrate that African Americans were *creators of* and *participants in* government. African Americans created the governmental structure and the positions in which members of the House now serve. Further, since the implied answers to Turner's rhetorical questions are "no," just as *humans* were not greater than *God*, or the "created greater than the Creator," so the Georgia Legislature (the created) and the positions within the Legislature were not greater than the African Americans who helped create them—and since they created them, they should serve as well.

Moreover, what Turner's opponents tried to do was analogous to a man entering Turner's house and taking possession of his wife and children and telling him to "get out." Turner's "house" is the Georgia *House* of Representatives. Turner's wife and children were analogous to his seat in the House. Thus, the analogy is clear: what Turner's opponents tried to do was to come into Turner's *House*, a house that he and other African Americans created, and take something that did not belong to them.

However, Turner discerned that there was something else at work. Turner and his opponents knew that to serve in the House meant that one had to speak, and there was a belief that black people could only speak "through white trumpets" or "white messengers." In other words, black people did not speak for themselves. For Turner it was a question of "manhood." Therefore, his rhetorical question, "Am I a man" spoke to the ontological nature of personhood.

The second set of opponents critiqued by Turner are the "Democrats." While "Anglo-Saxons" (whites) and "Democrats" would have been synonymous because "whites" in the Legislature were Democrats, Turner specifically called the "Democrats" by name because they were not only acting politically but ideologically as well because they led the charge to expel the African American members. Turner viewed this as an attack not only upon his person, but also upon his political party.

There are two specific references to the Democrats at the heart of Turner's critiques. The first came when Turner refuted the charge that African Americans have no right to hold office, which I have already discussed. The second critique came when Turner likened the Democrats to *Pharaoh* in the book of Exodus of the Bible.

> I say to you, *white men*, today, that the great deliverance of the recent past is not altogether dissimilar to the great deliverance of ancient times. Your *Democratic party* may aptly said [sic] to represent Pharaoh; the North to represent one of the walls, and the South the other. Between these two great walls the black man passes out to freedom, while your Democratic Party—the Pharaoh of to-day—follows us with hasty strides and lowering visage. (90, emphasis mine)

Although Turner spoke to the entire House and everyone else in the chamber that day, he specifically addressed "white men" and associated them with the Democratic Party—thus he critiqued the Democratic Party as a "white man's" political party that served the interest of white men. Moreover, grounded in the sacredness of a biblical story, Turner again not only adopted the moral high ground, which was intended to get his audience to reflect on their actions, but it also gave Turner a *safe place* to critique the Democrats. In the biblical story of the Exodus, the Israelites, released from bondage, head for freedom only to find out that Pharaoh and his army followed to enslave them again. The point Turner made was clear—the Democrats represented Pharaoh and black people represented Israel. As black people attempt to pass to freedom, the Democrats (Pharaoh) follow behind ready to enslave them again.

However, Turner's argument did something more. First, it represented African Americans as the ones who were victims of oppression and not whites who argued throughout the Reconstruction process that they were victims because of black political domination. Second and probably even more importantly, to be *Israel* in the story is also to be a *child of God*. Though Turner did not develop this line of thinking fully here, he definitely implied as much. Even though the Israelites were oppressed and placed in slavery, they were still the *children of God* and just as Israel received its freedom, African Americans, who were also children of God, had received their freedom and were walking towards that freedom despite resistance from the Democrats who were acting the part of Pharaoh.

Prophetic Warnings and Judgments

Since the Democrats oppressed African Americans ideologically and politically, Turner, as prophet, addressed these sins through warnings and judgment to his audience. There are two examples of this in Turner's speech. The first came near the end of the speech when Turner prophetically stated:

> You may expel us, gentlemen, but I firmly believe that you will some day repent it. . . . Go on with your oppressions. Babylon fell. Where is Greece? Where is Nineveh? And where is Rome, the mistress Empire of the world? Why is it that she stands, today, in the broken fragments throughout Europe? *Because oppression killed her*. Every act that we commit is like a bounding ball. If you curse a man, that curse rebounds upon you; and when you bless a man, the blessing returns to you; and when you oppress a man, the oppression will also rebound. . . . We are a persecuted people. Luther was persecuted; Galileo was persecuted; good men in all nations have been persecuted; but the persecutors have been handed down to posterity with shame and ignominy. (94-95, emphasis mine)

Turner offered a warning that if the House expelled African Americans they would "repent it." Turner drew from history and asked about the empires of the past rhetorically, "Where are they today?" His aim was clear—in the same way that Babylon, Greece, Nineveh, and Rome were guilty of oppression and injustice, so were the actions of Turner's opponents in the House. Therefore, not only was this an attack against African American personhood as Turner argued before, but it was also a form of blanket oppression.

Turner also warned his opponents that African Americans were a "persecuted people." To demonstrate this Turner presented both Luther and Galileo as good men who found themselves persecuted. The image here again was clear—Turner equated African American persecution to that of Luther and Galileo. Therefore, history would remember African Americans as innocent persecuted people as history has remembered Luther and Galileo for their innocent sufferings.

The second example of warning and judgment came right before the end of the speech.

> If you pass this Bill, you will never get Congress to pardon or enfranchise another rebel in your lives. . . . You may think you are doing yourselves honor by expelling us from this House; but when we go, we will do as Wickliffe [sic] and as Latimer did. We will light a torch of truth that will never be extinguished—the impression that will run through the country, as people picture in their mind's eye these poor black men, in all parts of this Southern country, pleading for their rights. When you expel us, you make us forever your political foes, and you will never find a black man to vote a Democratic ticket again: for, so help me, God, I will go through all the length and breadth of the land, where a man of my race is to be found, and advise him to beware of the Democratic party. Justice is the great doctrine taught in the Bible. God's Eternal Justice is founded upon Truth, and the man who steps from Justice steps from Truth, and cannot make his principles to prevail. (96)

Turner warned his opponents that if this bill passed, that they would never get Congress to "pardon another rebel." It was not an "honor" to expel the African Americans, but an act of rebellion and while the last act of rebellion led to some pardons, Congress would not pardon or enfranchise anyone else who was guilty of this infraction.[6]

In addition, the proposed House action gave Turner an opportunity to cast himself and his fellow African American representatives in another light. By invoking the names of Wycliffe and Latimer, Turner presented the African American members as *reformers*. Just as Wycliffe and Latimer were reformers, so too were the African American members reformers of sorts. As Wycliffe's and Latimer's reformation was one that centered on rights, so too was the African American's reformation—just as Wycliffe and Latimer did not give up, so too the African American representatives would not give up. In fact, according to Turner, taking another swipe at the dominant thinking of Anglo-Saxonism, the African Americans representatives would light a "torch of truth" for all to see, so that the world can see the "poor black man pleading for his rights."

Expulsion for Turner meant that African Americans would become enemies of the Democratic Party. Turner declared that he would make sure of that himself because truth was on his side. By adopting a prophetic persona, Turner had gone beyond the façade of his opponents' arguments. Knowing that he had to face racist thinking and ideology, he continued to believe that *truth* would prevail. For Turner, he found this truth in a God who not only cared about the oppressed but also, as we shall see, one who sought out justice for those oppressed.

Prophetic Hope and Encouragement

At first glance, there seems not to be any hope or optimism in this speech. Leeman writes in his critique of the speech:

> Turner was not optimistic; his public optimism had in this instance ebbed beyond recognition . . . the message of optimism was absent. Turner offered no message of hope for his audience even as he called upon them to repent, for he knew his audience, filled with unreconstructed Confederates and former slave holders, would not. (227)

However, adopting Leeman's position assumes that the only *audience* in the place that day was the "unreconstructed Confederates and former slave holders." African Americans were there as well. In addition, Leeman adopts an overtly restricted conception of audience. Turner, understanding that expulsion is a foregone conclusion, is not speaking primarily to his opponents—they have already rejected him and his arguments. Turner is speaking for the "ninety thousand black men—voters of Georgia," and Turner would continue to speak "until God, in His providence, shall see proper to take me hence," and he trusts that God "will give me the strength to stand, and the power to accomplish the simple justice that I see for them" (89).

By adopting a prophetic persona, Turner positions himself not in his opponents' community, but in the African American community. Understanding whom Turner claims to represent gives us a different perception of *audience*. Therefore, the question is not whether Turner offers hope and optimism, but how he does it for the African American audience he claims to represent.

> You may expel *us*, gentlemen, by *your* votes, today; but, while *you* do it, remember that there is a just God in heaven, whose All-seeing Eye beholds alike the acts of the oppressor and the oppressed, and who despite the machinations of the wicked, never fails to vindicate the cause of Justice, and the sanctity of His own handiwork. (96, emphasis mine)

Clearly, Turner is speaking on behalf of the African American members of the House when he speaks about "us" and "your." Turner knows there is nothing that he or his fellow members can do about expulsion. However, Turner does not leave *his* people hopeless. What Turner does is to invoke the presence of God who is in "heaven" and who has "all seeing eyes." The hope here is not that the House repents and changes its mind about expulsion. Nor is the hope that African Americans just trust in the "covenant" that Turner had lifted up in his *Emancipation Day* speech. The hope here is that God is watching and since God is watching and "never fails to vindicate the cause of Justice," it is that God will hear their pleas and rectify the situation.

Turner invited his African American audience to take a hopeless situation and see a ray of hope to help them continue to move forward. Expulsion was the fate of the African American members, and no matter how Turner or others spoke, their opponents did not hear them; they would not change their minds. Therefore, Turner invited his audience to remember that their opponents do not get the last word. The last word comes from a God who sits high, looks low, and will "vindicate the cause of justice," and is a call for African Americans to remain "just" and continue to wait on the Lord.

By the time Turner finished speaking, the verdict had all but been assured—the African American representatives were asked to give up their seats. It only took Turner two years to start questioning some of his earlier assumptions. In his *Emancipation Day* speech, Turner affirmed the *American Creed*, believing that America was the "stone cut from the mountain" from the biblical book of Daniel, and that America was ready to live up to its covenant. The *sacred* in that speech was America as *chosen* to lead the cause of liberty, and Turner would have believed this even more strongly because of his participation in Georgia governmental affairs and his becoming a leader in the Republican Party. While there was still prejudice and racism throughout the South during this time, Turner would have chalked that up to individual situations. He would not have accepted a systemic view of prejudice because he believed that America was the chosen nation and had taken on messiah-like qualities in spreading liberty, freedom, and justice throughout the world.

Turner's actions during this time reflected these assumptions. Angell wrote that Turner "did not advocate a free distribution of lands among the freed people," and he adhered to a "strict Puritan ethic, arguing that hard work would be suitably rewarded" (*Bishop* 63). Therefore, he held black business owners in high regard making sure in his letters to the *Christian Recorder* to offer a report about their successes. The rest of his time focused on building both the Republican Party in Georgia and the AME Church.

However, by 1868 Turner's views began to change. Still taking on the prophetic persona, Turner would no longer ground himself in the American creed. He would no longer believe that America itself was sacred and was the stone cut from the mountain for messianic purposes of somehow distributing liberty and freedom to all. Though he did draw upon the sacredness of the Constitution for political purposes in defining his manhood, what Turner did from this speech throughout the rest of his career was to appropriate the sacredness of God.

The other noticeable change in Turner's prophetic rhetoric was his conception of encouragement and hope. In his *Emancipation Day* speech, Turner saw the day where both blacks and whites could come together to make the South a better place for all. Turner saw blacks working hard and demonstrating their worth to whites, and he saw whites respecting blacks and receiving them into the larger society. The hope promoted in the speech was one of general unity where Turner acted as prophet of both communities.

In his *Eligibility* speech, Turner's hope was that God, seeing injustice, would act on the behalf of oppressed African Americans. This version of hope was not the inclusive one that Turner proclaimed in his *Emancipation Day* speech, but aimed at the people whom Turner represented. Turner's hope was that God would act because his opponents had already acted and acted not only in opposition to the American covenant, but also to God's will. Leeman is correct when he says that Turner's opponents rejected the American covenant, but Turner did not ground the speech in *this covenant*, but in the covenant that God has with all creation. It was that hope that African Americans could hold onto.

It was indeed this hope that God would act on their behalf that got the African Americans members, led by Turner, to go to Washington, D.C. and petition members of Congress for their seats in the House. By adopting the prophetic persona, Turner was able to offer another vision of hope that sustained, uplifted, strengthened, and encouraged African American members of the House and African Americans in general to keep moving and to keep hope alive.

However, as Turner and other African Americans, especially in the South, would soon discover, it would be hard for African Americans to keep hoping. There needed to be a plan, some sort of agenda—maybe a vision to go along with that hope. God would act if African Americans would demonstrate faith—not only in God, but also in themselves. Turner believed he was the one to present the vision where he saw God working on the behalf of African Americans—and that vision lead Turner to look not towards America, but to Africa.

Notes

1. Even though many preachers believed in the unity of humankind or that all humans came from the same source (God, through Adam and Eve), they still felt a need to rank the races. See Edward Hitchcock's *Religious Truth, Illustrated from Science, in Addresses and Sermons on Special Occasions* (Boston: Philips Samson and Company, 1857).

2. See Fredrick Douglass' 1852 speech "What, to a Slave, is the Fourth of July," in *Lift Every Voice and Sing: African American Oratory 1787-1900,* ed. Philip Foner and Robert James Branham (Univ. of Alabama Press, 1998).

3. It is interesting that Turner does not invoke the Thirteenth Amendment in his argument since he spent considerable time talking about slavery.

4. The Reconstruction measures that Turner addresses were the Civil Rights act of 1866, the Fourteenth Amendment, and the Georgia State Constitution.

5. For an example of a corrective on the myth of the docile Negro see "African Resistance to Enslavement: The Nature and the Evidentiary Record," *Journal of Black Studies* 23.1 (1992): 39-59.

6. In part of his attempt to work with Democrats and Conservatives, Turner supported the pardoning of former rebels including General Robert Lee.

Chapter Three

"To Seek Other Quarters": Turner's Mission-Oriented Prophecy

In August of 1893, Turner issued a call for African Americans to convene because for Turner, the time had come for blacks to consider emigrating out of
America. Turner wrote in the call:

> I do not believe that there is any manhood future in this country for the Negro,
> and that his future existence, to say nothing of his future happiness, will depend
> upon his nationalization. . . . But knowing that thousands and tens of thousands
> see our present conditions and our future about as I do, and after waiting for
> four years or more for some of our colored statesmen or leaders to call a na-
> tional convention or to propose some plan of speaking to the nation or to the
> world, or to project some measure that will remedy our condition, or will even
> suggest a remedy, and finding no one among the anti-emigrational party or an-
> ti-Negro nationalization party disposed to do so, and believing that further si-
> lence is not only a disgrace but a crime, I have resolved to issue a call in the
> near future for a national convention to be held in the city of Cincinnati, where
> a spacious edifice is at our disposal, to meet some time in November, for the
> friends of African repatriation or Negro nationalization elsewhere, to assemble
> and adopt such measures for our actions as may commend themselves to our
> better judgment. ("Colored," Aug. 1893)

Turner grounded the reason for the call in his belief that there was no personhood future in America for African Americans. At this point in his life, he
saw no way for African Americans to develop their own agency within the
boundaries of the United States. The country which he once believed was the
messianic hope for all oppressed people—"the stone cut from the mountain" in

71

the book of Daniel—has now, for Turner, become a place for oppression and suppression for African Americans.

In 1861 Turner, like many African Americans at the time, opposed emigration (Johnson, *Pastor* 12-14). However, according to Turner in a letter to the editor of the *Washington Post* in 1895, he became a "convert" to African emigration after hearing Alexander Crummell speak upon the subject in May 1862. While Turner may have inwardly thought about emigration during the time he spent in Washington, D.C., there is no textual evidence that he promoted emigration.

After the Civil War and the passage of the Thirteenth Amendment, Turner's interest in emigration began to wane because he now saw America as divinely inspired to promote liberty and justice for the oppressed. Though he wrote a letter to William Coppinger of the American Colonization Society in 1866 stating his support for emigration, evidence showed that Turner was busy promoting the virtues of hard work, self-reliance, blacks and whites working together and letting "bygones be bygones" (Redkey, *Respect* 13; Turner, *Emancipation*).

When Turner arrived in Savannah in 1872, he began thinking about emigration again. In his *Present Duties and the Future of the Negro Race* speech, Turner asserted that while he believed that African Americans would never be expatriated from America, black people one day will "turn [their] attention to Africa and go for it" (19). In his 1873 "Negro in All Ages" lecture, Turner argued that African Americans had a duty to civilize Africa and the only way he saw to do this is to "move into their midst and live among them" (29).

Turner's transformation did not come by accident. During his years in Savannah, Turner promoted the virtues of hard work, education, and African American success even under prejudice and racist conditions in 1873. However, during the next twenty years, three major incidents gave rise to Turner's advocacy of emigration.

With the Compromise of 1877 and the official end of Reconstruction, which effectively moved federal troops from the South, Democrats gained leadership in state governments by suppressing African American and white Republican votes. Turner became dismayed at this treatment and wrote an obituary for the Republican Party in which he felt betrayed, in part because of all the hard work he had done on behalf of the party. More specifically, he felt that the national Republican Party left Southern blacks to fend for themselves against the terrorist activity of the "Ku-Kluxers" (Angell 130).

With the election of many Democrats to state offices and along with the patronage given by national Republicans to Southern white Democrats as part of the Compromise, Southern blacks begin to talk about an exodus out of the South. Despite Pap Singleton's exodus movement in 1879, Turner did not feel the plan went far enough.[1] It lead Turner to develop a theory of emigration entitled *Emigration of the Colored People of the United States* that was read at the Colored National Convention held in Nashville on May 6, 1879. Although

Turner had "weaved Africa in his sermons and lectures" since 1866 (*Speeches and Writings* 12), he had never developed an overall reason for emigration—and while he advocated emigration much after this essay, it still stands as his only work devoted to the subject.

After a lengthy introduction of the history of emigration, Turner first argues that emigration "has the sanction from heaven and has been the theory, as well as a cardinal practice of all nations of antiquity." Second, he argues that emigration is a "pre-requisite to the material social and intellectual growth of a people," and as such, it is not "disgraceful, humiliating, or destructive to society." Finally, Turner argues that emigration is an honorable solution for a people who were "subjected to ill treatment, persecution, proscription, outrage and other forms of injustice" (*Emigration* 5).

Next, Turner addressed his African American critics—who argued that blacks should not be concerned with emigration to Africa or anywhere else because "colored people are to the manner born and, as such, are citizens of the United States" (*Emigration* 5). While attacking their arguments as illogical, Turner believed the problem many blacks had with emigration came from their dislike of the American Colonization Society (ACS). After refuting their arguments, Turner then addressed the questions of emigration—is it right; is it expedient?

Turner offered four primary reasons for emigration. First, African Americans should take pride in their homeland. Turner argued that all races of people take pride in their homelands and African Americans should be no different. Second, Africa's land and climate offers some of the best advantages for planting and farming. This appealed to black Southerners taken advantage of through the sharecropping system that sprang up after the Civil War. The third reason had to do with African American treatment in America. Turner argued that since African American treatment was based in black inferiority and oppression, African emigration provided a safe haven for blacks. Finally, Turner predicted "bad times" were ahead for America, which meant even worse times for African Americans.

After becoming bishop in 1880, the second incident that profoundly had an effect on Turner was the Supreme Court's decision declaring the 1875 Civil Rights Bill—which attempted to outlaw private discrimination in public spaces and places—unconstitutional. Turner was vigilant in his denunciation of the decision. Through an open letter to B.K. Sampson, who took an accommodationist approach to the Supreme Court decision—which was first printed in the *Memphis Appeal* then reprinted in the *Christian Recorder*—Turner believed the decision was "made in the interest of party politics"—meant to "drive the negro back into a line he thought he was deserting" (*CR* Dec. 13, 1883). Turner also argued that the decision "absolves the allegiance of the negro to the United States" and that if the "decision is correct, The United States Constitution is a dirty rag" it should be "spit upon by every negro in the land" and African

Americans should "prepare to return to Africa or get ready for extermination" (*CR* Dec. 13, 1883).

However, Turner's pamphlet *Civil Rights: The Outrage of the Supreme Court of the United States upon the Black Man. Reviewed in a Reply to the New York "Voice," The Great Temperance Paper of the United States,* criticizing the decision, gained widespread attention and circulation. Published six years after the decision in 1889, Turner's aim was to address Republican critics in defense of his accusation of the "Republican Supreme Court" allowing African Americans to be "turned out of hotels, cheated, abused and insulted on steamboats and railroads, without legal redress" (*Civil Rights* 2). The pamphlet not only included his reply to the editor of the *Voice*, but it also included a pastoral letter to the ministers and members of the eighth Episcopal district—the district in which he served as bishop.

The pastoral letter, written immediately after the decision, was conciliatory in tone. It counseled members of his district to do several things—first, discern, if any, the lesson God would have them learn from the decision. Second, to pray and fast for the reorganization of the Supreme Court as well as call meetings "by the thousands" and write petitions to Congress; and, to thank God for Justice Harlan—the lone dissenter of the decision, and other "friends of humanity" (*Civil Rights* 15).

However, while he struck a more pastoral tone with ministers and members of his district, Turner, with six years to see the effects of the decision, struck a more prophetic tone in his letter to the *Voice*. First, Turner argued that the decision was a farce because he believed that Justice Bradley (Chief Justice) and the "Republican Supreme Court" had "predetermined its non-constititutionality." What the Court could only see, argued Turner, was blacks and whites intermingling and associating with each other in hotels, inns, theatres, and on parlor cars. Turner argued that *these pictures* the Court did not want to see. Further, Turner wrote:

> Negroes may come as servants into all of the hotels, inns, theatres, and parlor-cars, but they never shall be received as equals—as are other persons. A negro woman with a white baby in her arms may go to the table in the finest and most aristocratic hotel, and there, as servant, be permitted to associate with all present, of whatever nationality. The same woman, unaccompanied by said baby, or coming without the distinguished rank of servant, is given to understand that she cannot enter. And what is more, by the Bradley infamous decision may be by force of arms prevented from entering. . . . The gambler, cut-throat, thief, despoiler of happy homes, and the cowardly assassin, need only to have white faces in order to be accommodated with more celerity and respect than our lawyers, doctors, teachers and humble preachers. (*Civil Rights* 7)

For Turner, whites were concerned with how *whites and black intermingled* and the intermingling could only happen in a servant-master relationship. As long as blacks were in the role of servants, they could associate with all present—however, when they intermingled without a badge of inferiority, blacks found themselves barred from entering the cars or simply cheated out of their rightful positions as social equals. Turner makes this clear when he writes:

> I am charged by your Pennsylvania correspondent with saying that, "By the decision of the Republican Supreme Court, colored people may be turned out of hotels, cheated, abused and insulted on steamboats and railroads, without legal redress." I am of the opinion that the reporter on your paper, who published the above quotation as coming from me, made no mistake, unless it was that of making it more mild than I intended. When I used the term "cheated," I mean that colored persons are required to pay first-class fare and in payment there for are given no-class treatment, or at least the kind with which no other human being, paying first class fare is served. (*Civil Rights* 7)

After praising dissenting Justice Marshall and quoting major pieces of his dissent, Turner then turned his attention to the 1875 Civil Rights bill. For Turner, the Court acted with "wicked ingeniousness and color-phobism" because they knew Congress intended to "entirely free" and not "partly liberate" African Americans.

> The desire was to remove the once slave so far from his place of bondage, that he would not even remember it, if such a thing were possible. Congress stepped in and said, he shall vote, he shall serve on juries, he shall testify in court, he shall enter the professions, he shall hold offices, he shall be treated like other men, in all places the conduct of which is regulated by law, he shall in no way be reminded by partial treatment, by discrimination, that he was once a "chattel," a "thing." (*Civil Rights* 10)

Turner's argument for his position came from his belief that Congress had a right to do this because "the power that made him the slave a man instead of a 'thing' had the right to fix his status." Turner believed that the "height of absurdity, the chief point of idiocy, the brand of total imbecility, is to say, that the Negro shall vote a privilege into existence which one citizen may enjoy for pay, to the exclusion of another." He also wondered, "Are colored men to vote grants to railroads upon which they cannot receive equal accommodation?" (*Civil Rights* 10). Moreover, for Turner, God was not pleased with the Republicans because the year after the decision, the Democrats defeated the Republicans in the national elections because "God would have men do right, harm no one, and to render to every man his just due" (*Civil Rights* 11).

Further invoking God and acknowledging that the LORD OF HOSTS REIGNS, Turner wrote:

> God may forgive this corps of unjust justices, but I never can, their very memories will also be detested by my children's children, nor am I alone in this detestation. The eight millions of my race and their posterity will stand horror-frozen at the very mention of their names. The scenes that have passed under my eyes upon the public highways, the brutal treatment of helpless women I have witnessed, since the decision was proclaimed, is enough to move heaven

to tears and raise a loud acclaim in hell over the conquest of wrong. (*Civil Rights* 12)

For Turner the message was clear—more than just a decision, this was an all-out attack against African Americans to disassociate them from society, removing any gains they may have made through the passing of the Thirteenth, Fourteenth, and Fifteenth Amendments. Not only did he feel that African Americans were under attack, but they were under attack by supposed friends—the Republican Party. As Turner made clear, previous Republican presidents stacked the Supreme Court with Republican appointees; therefore, this became a *Republican* position on race relations—races should remain separate and states have the rights to enforce this belief.

After the publication of *Civil Rights,* the third incident that transformed Turner was when he finally realized his dream and traveled to Africa in 1891. The AME Church had made some overtures in Liberia because several pastors of the denomination had immigrated to Africa. Therefore, Turner's travels ostensibly helped further establish those existing churches. However, Turner used this opportunity to not only fulfill his duties as bishop, but also he wanted to know first hand if Africa was all that he had been proclaiming. Turner wrote as he prepared for his trip:

> My chief object in going to Africa is to organize some mission conferences and ordain a number of ministers for the mission work of our church. I will also look over the ground with reference to my plan. If God spare my life to return, I shall let the country know what my conclusions are. (*Respect Black* 84)

While in Africa, Turner kept his word and wrote letters chronicling his trip. These letters, first published in the *Christian Recorder* and later published as a pamphlet entitled *African Letters,* gave readers his views about Africa. Most noticeable in the letters was Turner's surprise at the continent itself. In describing Sierra Leone, Turner wrote:

> I thought it was a low, swampy lagoony town, with narrow, muddy streets, as filthy as a cesspool; but cleanliness, pavements sidewalks, rock-sewers and decency everywhere met the eye. But when I pointed this and that fine building out, and was told that they all belong to black men, I was surprised more than ever. Again, when I inquired about the great cathedral, with tower and clock, and other large churches, with spires, domes and steeples, and was told they were black people's churches, I had to say, thank God for this sight! (*African Letters* 33)

In writing about Liberia Turner states:

> Liberia is one of the most paradisiacal portions of earth my eyes ever beheld. Any person who cannot live here with reasonable health cannot exist anywhere. . . . How under heaven some Negroes can come here and after remaining awhile, go back to America and give this place a bad name I cannot understand.

. . . This is the only country I have ever seen where everybody could have a stream of water running through his yard. It is the most perfectly watered region I have ever witnessed. (*African Letters* 52)

After his trip to Africa, Turner believed the time was right to start seriously promoting his vision of emigration. With the rising tide of white supremacy, Turner seriously believed that things were not going to get better for blacks and that emigration was the only viable option. In a letter to the editor of the *Indianapolis Freedman* Turner wrote, "I have said, and say yet, that there is no more hope for the black man in this country to become a civil and political factor, than there is for a frog in a snake den. And any man who is too idiotic to see it ought to go and hang himself" (quoted in *Respect Black* 136). Therefore, Turner started to engage in an African emigration campaign.

Turner had two major things working in his favor as he prepared his campaign on emigration. First, the American Colonization Society was constantly receiving letters of inquiry and applications for trips to Africa and promised to offer as many trips as the Society possibly could, and second, many were creating emigration clubs especially throughout the South and out West. Redkey acknowledged that many attributed much of this excitement to the violence and economic depression of many Southern blacks, but much of the credit must go to Turner's "long campaign, punctuated by his glowing letters" from Africa (*Black Exodus* 172). Many who wrote to the Society mentioned Turner by name and many waited "eagerly to hear more about the Promised Land" from Turner (*Black Exodus* 172).

When the Colonization Society ceased publication of the *African Repository* at the end of 1892, Turner picked up the mantle to become the leading advocate for emigration. First, in January of 1893, Turner created *The Voice of Missions*. Ostensibly a publication of the AME Church with the stated purpose of "popularizing missionary activity and encouraging donations for converting the heathen" (*Black Exodus* 177), with Turner as editor, the newspaper quickly became the unofficial propaganda sheet for African emigration.

Although the paper contained news about wider church activities, through editorials, letters, and features, it vigorously proposed African emigration for American blacks. By the end of its first year the journal had achieved a reported monthly circulation of over 4,000. Because most of these papers were read by pastors of AME churches throughout the South, their message reached far more people than the circulation figures might suggest. The monthly proved to be an effective vehicle for Turner's propaganda. (*Black Exodus* 177)

After launching the paper, Turner set sail again for Africa. The reason for the second trip was to "answer appeals of the African people for help in evangelizing the natives and strengthening their churches" (*Black Exodus* 179). However, just like his first trip to Africa, the second one had a dual purpose as well.

Not only was Turner interested in helping evangelize Africans, but also he was very interested in finding support for an American-African trade connection.

However, on his second trip to Africa, Turner noticed a major difference—he noticed more white people. The presence of white people going to Africa to "exploit a silver mine" or "encroach the border" for a hostile takeover, bothered Turner. He argued that white control "might destroy his African dream" and pleaded with blacks and whites alike that "Africa be saved for the Africans" (*Black Exodus* 180).

> Since my arrival here I find that white immigration to Africa has greatly increased. If the United States should stop the great tide of immigration there, as is thought here will be done, Africa is gone and the black race will have no home upon the face of the globe. (*Respect Black* 140)

However, the trip to Africa also offered Turner another opportunity to write glowing and flattering opinions about Africa. This time, his letters found publication in both the *Christian Recorder* and *Voice of Mission*. About Turner's letters, Redkey noted that:

> Turner letters were full of overstated praise for Africa and criticism for blacks who were letting a great opportunity slip through their fingers. The simple fact that the great advocate of emigration was writing directly from Africa drew enthusiastic responses from many Southern blacks, as was indicated by letters to the press and to the Colonization Society. On his return the bishop reinforced that interest by constantly lecturing and writing about Africa. . . . As a propaganda junket, the trip was a success. (*Black Exodus* 181)

The third part of his campaign was his invitation to speak at the Columbian Exposition at Chicago. At the exposition, there was a weeklong Congress on Africa. Attendance for the Congress was good and attendees presented speeches and papers on Africa. In what Redkey says "shocked whites and pleased blacks" was Turner's participation in the discussion of "The African in America." In that discussion, Turner announced that the first man, Adam, was in fact black. Turner's positions and outspokenness got him coverage from the *Chicago Tribune* that also included a portrait of Turner and a summary of his emigration views (*Black Exodus* 182).

For Turner, the Chicago exposition served his interests in several ways. First, it gave him a wider platform for African propaganda. Second, the coverage in the white-owned *Chicago Tribune* helped Turner reach a larger audience and gave him some credibility in the larger society. Third, he convinced some former outright opponents of emigration to modify their positions by endorsing a plan to allow only a "qualified few to go." Fourth, Turner and the other presenters had the chance at the exposition to educate many blacks on Africa.

However, it would be the fourth part of Turner's campaign that would be the most challenging—calling a national convention with the express purpose of discussing African emigration. Due to the encouraging and supportive responses of his earlier efforts and with increased lynching, erosion of black civil rights, and the threat of European colonization in Africa, Turner believed that the time was right to call for a national black convention that would produce some radical action and for Turner, this meant emigration to Africa.

After his initial call for the convention, the response was overwhelming. Turner wrote in the *Voice of Missions* that "over three-hundred responsible Negroes had endorsed the call and delegates from all over the world would attend" (*Black Exodus* 185). Even though Turner called for a *Black National Convention*, the convention took on the name "Turner's Convention."

However, Turner still faced rhetorical hurdles. First, Turner had to face the *North/South dichotomy*. Many blacks in the North favored staying in America and trying to appeal to whites for justice and equality. They claimed their American citizenship and expected other blacks to do so as well. In addition, many blacks in the North were middle-class blacks who had made some upward progress during Reconstruction. Albeit still troubled by racism and prejudice, Redkey notes that "American individualism had begun to bear fruit for them and, despite their belonging to the black caste; they had risen in wealth and education above the masses of plantation workers" (*Black Exodus* 30). Blacks in the North felt as if they had more to lose on a risky venture such as emigration whereas Southern blacks thought, "it could not be worse than it already is for us now."

The second rhetorical hurdle Turner had to face was the strong myths associated with Africa. Many blacks had questions about the "suitability of the Dark Continent" based upon "ignorance, misinformation, and the grim accounts of some disillusioned travelers" (*Black Exodus* 38). There was major concern about the climate and the unbearable heat, which many believed led to incurable fevers and all kinds of diseases. It also did not help Turner when some emigrants returned from Africa with horror stories of death and disease and talked about the many swamps of inhabitable land in Africa. Even whites, concerned that a ready labor supply was interested in possible emigration to Africa, started spreading rumors about African slavery (*Black Exodus* 38).

Third, as much as Turner spoke and wrote concerning the merits of emigration, others were speaking and writing against emigration. By 1883, "black churchmen and secular leaders who were optimistic about the United States began to attack Turner's emigration schemes in the *Christian Recorder* (*Black Exodus* 30-31).

The *Christian Recorder* published much opposition to emigration plans. Many of the *Recorder's* writers felt that emigration was too great a price to pay for social equality. Some made the argument that blacks are Americans and have no affinity towards Africa. Frederick Douglass reminded *Recorder* readers that blacks had "been in America for 250 years" and owed nothing to Africa. Douglass believed that America provided the best place for blacks to achieve equality (quoted in *Black Exodus* 32).

Fourth, was the characterization by Northern blacks of Southern blacks. Knowing that Turner's appeals for emigration resonated with Southern blacks, some Northern blacks started a campaign that elevated their status and reminded each other that they were the ones who were literate versus the illiterate black people in the South. Following this logic, Benjamin Tanner, editor of the *Christian Recorder* wrote since he "knew the thoughts of those Negroes who could read and write, what one thoughtful man among us writes outweighs in value the whole Niagara of eloquence common to our people [who] talk in the vein that we know our hearers desire us to talk" ("Bishop Turner" 4 Jan. 1883). He was also critical of Turner for hearing only what he wanted to hear and not really listening to his own people.

Tanner also pointed out that while Turner espoused leaving America, many people were already coming to America to fulfill dreams in the land of opportunity. Tanner also reminded his readers that even Africans who come to America to study usually stay in America after their studies are completed. Tanner wrote in the *Recorder*, "The idea of a people leaving a country like America to go anywhere to better their condition . . . is like running from the sun for both light and heat" ("Turner's Reply" 2 Feb. 1883).

Despite the negative reactions to emigration, Turner forged ahead with the convention. At the start of the convention, the attendance was better than Turner expected. About eight hundred delegates registered along with many local blacks from the host city Cincinnati who all came to hear the emigration-minded bishop speak. However, when Turner stood to speak he knew that the majority of attendees did not support his call for emigration. Therefore, what rhetorical strategy did Turner use to invite his audience to consider his agenda? I suggest that he adopted a prophetic persona of a pragmatic prophet and issued a (re)constitutive rhetoric that I call mission-oriented prophecy that called his primarily African American audience to a divine purpose.

Turner's "Negro Convention" Speech

Grounded in the Sacred

At the beginning of the speech, Turner grounds it in *divine mystery*. After declaring that the United States has "decitizentized" African Americans with the Supreme Court ruling that the 1875 Civil Rights Bill was unconstitutional, Turner lays the foundation of his (re)constitutive rhetoric by declaring

> While it is true we were brought here as captive heathens, through the greed and avarice of the white man, to serve him as a slave, I believe that as *overruling Providence* suffered it to be because there was a *great and grand purpose to be subserved*, and that infinite wisdom intended to involved ultimate good out of temporary evil, and that in ages to come, the glory of God will be made manifest and that millions will thank heaven for the limited toleration of

American slavery. All of you may not accept my sentiments upon this point, *but I believe there is a God, and that he takes cognizance of human events; for such a stupendous evil could not have existed so long, affecting the destiny of the unborn, without a glorious purpose in view.* ("Negro," Dec. 1893, emphasis mine)

With this paragraph, Turner not only grounded his speech in the Providence of God to bring out of a "temporary evil" the "glory of God," but he also attempted to reconstitute a collective subject. Of course, the collective subject here was "African Americans," and Turner could have called them into being by invoking American citizenship and claiming the rights and privileges associated with citizenship. However, Turner cannot do this because he believed that America had *revoked citizenship* from African Americans when he stated earlier,

Let us, by the way of premises, itemized a few facts connected with our career in this country. We have been inhabitants of this continent for 273 years, and a very limited part of that time we were citizens—I mean from the ratification of the XIV amendment of the national constitution until the Supreme Court of the United States, Oct. 15th, 1883, declared that the provision of the constitution null and void, and decitizentized us. ("Negro")

Of course, Turner could not have meant literally that America had revoked citizenship from African Americans. However, what Turner attempted to do with his "decitizentized" statement was to place his audience in a position that allowed them to reach back to the past. Therefore, arguing that African Americans had been "decitizentized," Turner can now reach back to the past to a time when African Americans were not *citizens*. By invoking the slavery narrative and all that is to follow, Turner attempted to reconstitute his audience by positing the subject of slavery historically. By linking the past to the present, Turner wanted his audience to see themselves as "decitizentized" (as slaves) instead of as "citizens." If the audience did this, then they might join Turner in his reinterpretation of slavery.

Many saw slavery as a "school of correction" for the "elevation" of the Negro (Smith 143). In other words, a majority of whites and a large number of blacks saw slavery as rescuing blacks from the savages of Africa to introduce them to Christianity. Many in Turner's audience that day and many who would read the speech the following month would have had adopted this belief. However, Turner prophetically challenged this thinking.

While maintaining the sovereignty of God, Turner challenged this belief in two ways. First, slavery happened because of the "greed and avarice" of the white man. In other words, slavery was purely about economics. Whites did not want a school of instruction, nor did they want to expose slaves to Christianity.[2] For Turner, slavery was about money.

Second, by grounding himself in the belief of an "over-ruling Providence," Turner saw an "ultimate good" where the "glory of God will be made manifest," even to the point that "millions will thank heaven for the limited toleration of American slavery." While "millions" was an example of hyperbole, we should note Turner's rhetorical effort. What Turner did was to place slavery back into the hands of God—being careful not to blame God for slavery—the blame goes to the "greed and avarice of the white man"—but to acknowledge that God was at work even during the evils of slavery. In other words, God did not abandon African Americans during slavery, and by extension God will not abandon African Americans now. What God was doing was bringing good out of evil. Therefore, Turner's God is a God who works in evil situations by bringing out a "glorious purpose."[3]

Turner would address the "glorious purpose" later, but here Turner has two objectives that set the foundation for the rest of the speech. First, by declaring that African Americans were *not citizens*, Turner wanted to link the present to the past by reminding his audience of the ordeal of slavery and second, by reinterpreting slavery as an evil that could produce some good, Turner rhetorically sets up his audience to participate in the "glorious purpose."

The Sharing of the Real Situation

Turner shares truth in two major ways. First, Turner engages in *recall*. Recall acts as a reminder to the audience of something they already know. Therefore, placing recall in context with Charland, recall narratives act as transhistorical subjects. In this long recall, Turner states:

> As slaves we were obedient, faithful, and industrious. We felled the forests, tilled the ground, pioneered civilization and were harmless. . . . The first blood that crimsoned the soil for American independence was the blood of the negro, Crispus Attucks, in the tea riot in the streets of Boston. Over five thousand Negro patriots fought in the Revolutionary War for freedom from British domination and American independence. General Jackson issued an official proclamation complimenting the bravery and patriotism of black men in the war of 1812 at the battle of New Orleans. 185,000 negro soldiers came to the defense of the stars and stripes in the late internecine war between the North and the South, and 46,000 of them are now sleeping in bloody graves for the integral unity of a nation that cares nothing for them. . . . Singular and strange as it may appear to some present, a black man completed the Goddess of Liberty, which ornaments the dome of our national capitol; and it will stand there, heaven high, as a monument to his genius and industry for ages to come. Yet this same Goddess of Liberty has been transformed into a lying strumpet, so far as she symbolizes the civil liberties of the black man. ("Negro")

Usually the recall functions rhetorically three ways. First, it brings back to remembrance the achievements and accomplishments of a "people." Second, it links the past and the present and finally, since the audience knows the story, it allows the speaker to identify with the audience and share in its values. However, the recall usually is not an "innocent retelling" of an historical situation. It is a rhetorically strategic retelling of history, meant to get the audience not only to agree to what *is being said*, but also to *become a part of what is being said*. In short, placing recall in Charland's context, it is the beginning of interpellation.

Notice Turner's language with this recall. "As slaves . . . we were obedient, faithful, and industrious." He could have said, as slaves "*they were,*" but by using the inclusive "we," Turner means to identify with the slaves of history and by extension, Turner wants his audience to identify with the slaves as well. Turner has already set this attempt of interpellation earlier by calling African American "decitizentized." In other words, just as slaves were non-citizens, his audience also was non-citizens.

However, these "non-citizens" were "obedient, faithful, and industrious." In other words, these slaves carried with them some admirable qualities. This was important to note because many whites believed at this time that African Americans were lazy, shiftless, unfaithful, and unseemly. However, what was more damaging to the psyche of African Americans was the fact that many black people had internalized this thinking as well. Turner was attempting to show that even while in slavery, blacks had character, resolve, and fortitude. These character traits extended to the nation's wars. By invoking the bravery of the African Americans during wartime, Turner reminded his audience of the bravery of "non-citizens," people who served and protected a country that cared "nothing for them."

The connection that Turner attempted to make between the slaves (non-citizens) and his audience was that these people (slaves) were people who took action within their situations. Instead of being a passive people who looked for whites to do and be everything in their lives, these "non-citizens" took matters into their own hands. By having these character traits and by being an industrious "people," slaves forged their own way and earned their freedom. In short, nobody gave these people anything. It was their hard work and ingenuity that brought them freedom, and by invoking the inclusive "we" Turner implied that his audience and the slaves share in this same work ethic and destiny.

The second way that Turner shares truth was when he spoke about lynching. Turner takes up more than half the speech on this topic because due to Ida B. Wells' publication *Southern Horrors: Lynch Law in All Phases* in 1892, lynching had become a major concern for African Americans. While many in his audience would have already known about the lynching that was taking place, Turner's reasoning for invoking it is much deeper than just to remind his audiences of the horrors of lynching.

First, Turner strategically placed his words on lynching within the context of the speech. They come right after Turner critiqued the nation for not being faithful to African Americans as much as African American have been faithful to the nation. Then he said,

> Nevertheless, freedom had been so long held up before us as a man's normal birthright, and as the bas-relief of every possibility belonging to the achievements of manhood, that we received it as heaven's greatest boon and *nursed*

ourselves into satisfaction, believing that we had the stamina, not only to wring existence out of poverty, but also wealth, learning, honor, fame, and immortality. ("Negro," emphasis mine)

In the above passage, Turner critiqued his audience by accusing them of nursing themselves into satisfaction by believing that freedom would be the answer to all of their problems. The people had held up freedom as "man's normal birthright" and African Americans received it as "heaven's greatest boon" believing that they had the fortitude to wring "existence out of poverty." In other words, African Americans thought that freedom was automatically going to produce the conditions that promote a healthy "life" or "well-being," but as Turner would later note, this has not happened.

Remembering that when the prophet tells of the real situation or shares truth, she or he means to share information with the audience that the audience already knows, Turner shares this information, not to educate his audience, but prophetically to *name the demon*. By hearing the abuses of lynching, Turner's audience can agree with him that not only this is an injustice, but also each lynching that goes unsolved strips African Americans of their dignity.

The second way that the lynching part of the speech functions rhetorically was the way that Turner used it to expose degradation. First, if black men were raping white women, it was because whites were degrading African Americans. After mentioning the only raping incident involving a black man in the West Indian Islands, Turner said:

> It may be, however, due to the fact that there the laws and institutions recognize the black man as a full-fledged citizen and a gentleman and his pride of character and sense of dignity are not degraded and self-respect imparts a higher prompting and gentlemanly bearing to his manhood, and makes him a better citizen and inspires him with more gallantry and nobler principles. For like begets like. While in this country we are degraded by the public press, degraded by class legislation, degraded on the railroads after purchasing first class tickets, degraded at hotels and barbershops, degraded in many states at the ballot box, degraded in most large cities by being compelled to rent houses in alleys and the most disreputable streets. Thus we are degraded in so many respects that all the starch of respectability is taken out of the manhood of millions of our people, and as degradation begets degradation, it is very possible that in many instances we are guilty of doing a series of infamous things that we would not be guilty of, if our environments were different. ("Negro")

Second, if blacks were guilty of raping white women, Turner asked about the supposed justice.

> Under the genius and theory of civilization throughout the world, no man is guilty of a crime, whatever, until he is arrested, tried by an impartial process of the law and deliberately convicted. . . . Lynching a man is an act of barbarism and cannot be justified by even what a distinguished bishop terms "emotional

insanity." For even insanity has no authority to intrude its maddened vengeance upon the law and order of the public. ("Negro")

What Turner did was to place the burden of raping (if indeed this was happening), not on black men, but on whites. In the first example, he linked rape with the *inability* of blacks to be "full-fledge citizens." Note that the inability was not on the part of black people but on whites. Moreover, if rapes were occurring, it was because society treated blacks in such a degrading position that African Americans could not attain self-respect or a sense of dignity. For Turner, when the "starch of respectability" has been removed from the "manhood" of a "people," then it was very possible that blacks could be guilty of doing things that they would not do if the situations and "environments were different."

In the second example, Turner called upon the "genius and theory of civilization." Under this scenario, if black men raped white women, the accused still deserved a fair and impartial trial. This did not happen because of the "barbarianism" of lynching. In other words, for Turner, lynching went against the "genius and theory of civilization," and was insane and a "maddened vengeance upon the law and order of the public." In short, Turner claimed that America was not civilized and a place where African Americans were not safe, because America allowed this to happen.

Charge, Challenge, Critique, Judgment and/or Warning

While Turner filled his speech with many critiques and challenges, he focused a large portion of the speech on two groups. First, he critiqued his audience or blacks in general by challenging his audience. If rapes were happening, Turner argued that the people must do something about the situation.

> If the charges are true, then God has no attribute that will side with us. Nature has no member, no potential factor that will defend us, and while we may not all be guilty, nor one in ten thousand, it nevertheless shows, if true, that there is a libidinous taint, a wanton and lecherous corruption that is prophetic of a dreadful doom, as there must be a carnal blood poison in the precincts of our race that staggers the most acute imagination in determining its woeful results. There is but one recourse left us that will command the respect of the civilized world and the approval of God, and that is to investigate the facts in the premises, and if guilty, acknowledge it and let us organize against the wretches in our own rank. ("Negro")

Who should do something? Not society, who had already demonstrated incivility through the terrorist tactic of lynching, but African Americans themselves should do something about this supposed situation. What Turner attempted to do by way of critique was to challenge his audience to take control and use their agency and within their own communities stop the violence perpetrated against women (if indeed violence happened). In other words, Turner was prophetically calling his audience to take control of their own situations as *"non-citizens"* did prior to Emancipation. Turner wanted his audience to forge their own way that would empower and uplift the community.

By grounding this critique in the sacred (God), Turner also showed the degree of seriousness that his audience should demonstrate. For Turner, if the charges of rape are true, then even God will not be on their side. However, there is hope. If African Americans are vigilant in "investigating the facts" (doing something) and acknowledge any wrongdoing, then the people will have the approval of God. By couching his critique this way, Turner assumed the role of prophet/priest. If guilty of the sin of rape, Turner called his audience to find the culprits and admit the sin. By doing this, he offered absolution for the sin so that African Americans could get the "approval of God." This was why he could later thunder:

> Let us call upon the colored ministry to sound it from the pulpit, our newspapers to brand it with infamy daily, weekly, monthly, and yearly. Let us put a thousand lecturers in the field and canvass every section of the land, and denounce the heinous crime. Let us organize ourselves into societies, associations, and reforming bands, and let them hold public meetings, print circulars and awaken among our young men a better sentiment. ("Negro")

After sharing his concerns about lynching, Turner turns his attention to a scathing critique of America. The critique comes in two parts—first in a prophetic warning to the nation, and second in judgment that America does not have any desire to include African Americans in the covenantal promises of America.

Turner's warning sounds apocalyptic. "Unless this nation," Turner warned, "awakes from its slumber and calls a halt to the reign of blood and carnage in the land, its dissolution and utter extermination is only a question of a short time." Turner lists other countries—Egypt, Greece, Babylon, Nineveh, and Rome—that were "numerically stronger than the United States" that "went down" and he prophetically foresees the time when America will also *go down* unless it changes its ways ("Negro").

Turner argued that America was doomed because of the way it treated African Americans. Turner warned that though African Americans were a "very small item in the body politic," their groans, prayers and innocent blood will speak to God day and night" and that the "God of the poor and helpless will come to African Americans relief sooner or later." This relief, Turner argued would come in another "fratricide war" though he admits it may "grow out of an issue as far from the Negro as midday is from midnight" ("Negro").

Here Turner leaves room for a chance of African Americans becoming part of the covenantal promise of America. The nation has a chance to *wake up* and stop the "blood and carnage." The nation has a chance to live up to the ideals espoused in the covenant and offer African Americans full equality and citizenship. However, failure to do this will result in America suffering the fate of other countries in the past—countries that also affirmed the "spirit of conquest, cruelty, and injustice"—because the prayers and cries of African Americans that speaks to "God day and night" ("Negro").

By framing his argument this way, Turner opened a potentially powerful rhetorical space that would have allowed him to continue down an *apocalyptic road* of freedom. Framing African Americans as the children of Israel who cried out to God to deliver them from Pharaoh, Turner created a space for his audience to wait on supernatural deliverance from God when in due time everything will work itself out. Undoubtedly this has been the strategy of many African American orators during this time—a vision of an apocalyptic drama that sets things right.

However, Turner does not opt for this vision. Turner sees this as a flawed vision primarily for two reasons. First, for restoration to happen, America must *wake up* from its "slumbers" and stop the "reign of blood and carnage." In other words, order comes when America repents of its *lynching spirit,* and Turner sees no evidence of America repenting or abating the lynching of African Americans. Second, if America does not repent and change its "program," America will fall and that would affect everybody—including African Americans.

To support his argument, Turner presents a bitter critique of America's treatment of African Americans. When speaking about the lack of protection that African Americans have in the United States, Turner states:

> The truth is, the nation as such, has no power or disposition to give us manhood protection anyway. Congress had constitutional power to pursue a runaway slave by legislation into any state and punish the man who would dare conceal him and the Supreme Court of the United States sustained its legislation as long as slavery existed. Now the same Supreme Court has the power to declare that the Negro has no civil rights under the general government that will protect his citizenship, and authorize the states to legislate upon and for us, as they may like; and they are passing special acts to degrade the Negro by authority of the said tribunal, and Congress proposes no remedy by legislation or by such a constitutional amendment as will give us the status of citizenship in the nation that is presumed we are to love and to sacrifice our lives, if need be, in the defense of. ("Negro")

Turner started his critique by announcing *truth.* Grounded in his prophetic persona, truth for Turner was that America did not want to give African Americans protection *anyway.* By offering this declaration, Turner suggested that America could offer protection for African Americans if it wanted to do so. For Turner, the problem was in the *desire of the country* to offer these protections to African Americans—and to view them as citizens. Turner exposed the hypocrisy of the nation and its institutions. The height of hypocrisy was that the nation claimed the authority to protect slave owners by giving "constitutional power" to pursue runaway slaves but did not claim that same authority to protect African Americans.

With this critique, Turner also exposed something else. By not having constitutional rights and thereby not being citizens of America, Turner suggested that African Americans were at the mercy of states to pass legislation. However, states intend their legislation to "degrade" African Americans by "authority of the said high tribunal." What Turner wanted to make clear was that without federal protection, states run amok and trample on the rights of African Americans. Moreover, he also wanted his audience to know that the degrading of African Americans was part of a long-term plan aimed at making African Americans feel inferior and inadequate. Moreover, according to Turner, there was no remedy because Congress and the Supreme Court participated in the degradation by giving the states the authority to pass degrading laws.

To emphasize his point Turner states:

> Yet Congress can legislate for the protection of the fish in the sea and the seals that gambol in our waters, and obligate its men, its money, its navy, its army and its flag to protect, but the 8,000,000 or 10,000,000 of its black men and women, made in the image of God, possessing $265,000,000 worth of taxable property, with all their culture, refinement in many cases, and noble bearing, must be turned off to become the prey of violence, and when we appeal to the general government for protection and recognition, Justice, so-called, drops her scales and says, away with you. ("Negro")

Turner's goal was clear—he wanted his audience to consider the position in which America has placed African Americans. While America protected wildlife, it cannot protect its "black men and women" who "possess property," and who are "made in the image of God." Once again by invoking the *sacred,* Turner makes the accusation that this was not only wrong politically but it is also wrong morally. Therefore, the sin of racism needed examination and its demon exorcised. However, for Turner this will not happen because, as he said earlier, America "has no disposition" to give African Americans any kind of protection concerning their civil rights.

Therefore, in Turner's vision, African Americans find themselves in a serious dilemma. On the one hand, they can remain in America and keep their "present ignoble status, with the possibility of being shot, hung or burnt," for crimes they did or did not commit, or they can physically resist by taking up arms. Turner argues that the former option would declare African Americans "unfit to be free men or to assume the responsibilities which involve fatherhood and existence," while the latter was "literal madness." Turner reasoned that the idea that African Americans can take on whites in a race war is insane because of the financial and numerical strength of whites and so it is "folly to indulge in such a thought for a moment" ("Negro"). What then can African Americans do within Turner's somber vision of America? Where is the hope?

Encouragement and Hope

By framing his argument as an either/or proposition, Turner opened an avenue for a third option. Turner's rhetorical aims were clear—he wanted the audience to see their predicament as hopeless, thereby giving him an opportunity to proclaim prophetic hope by way of emigration. He did this first by acknowledging that African Americans wanted and desired hope in a hopeless situation when he proclaimed, "I know that thousands of our people hope and expect better times for the Negro in this country." However, Turner saw "no signs of a reformation" in the condition of African Americans. "To the contrary" he argued, "we are being more and more degraded by legislative enactments and judicial decisions." While acknowledging that promoting education and the erecting of some schools have helped, Turner bemoaned, "a hundred things have been done to crush out the last vestige of self-respect and to avalanche us with contempt" ("Negro").

While Turner knew many African Americans hoped for a brighter future in America, he argued that it was a false hope because of their condition. Not only had lynching and public opinion stifled African Americans, but they also had to contend with legislative and judicial prejudices. In essence Turner, by adopting a prophetic persona, saw behind the curtain—that the oppression of African Americans was total and that everyone was involved: the people, the government and the courts of law. In short, as long as African Americans remained in America, degradation of African Americans would continue because *society* believed in the inferiority of African Americans.

Therefore, Turner suggests the solution. "My remedy," Turner declares, "without a change, is, as it would be folly to attempt resistance and our appeals for better conditions are being unheeded, for that portion of us, at least who feel we are self-reliant to seek other quarters" ("Negro"). Owing to the make-up of his audience, Turner chooses his words carefully. Turner says, "My remedy without a change." Here Turner seems to give space to the prospect of staying in America—if America changes. While this seems at first an opening to work for better conditions in America and produce the desired change, Turner has already declared that possibility moot. Thus, this opening statement of his plan acts to convince his audience that change is not actually coming forth. Since it is "folly to attempt resistance" and the "appeals for better conditions are being unheeded," Turner has already dismissed both of those options, leaving only one answer.

Turner's answer was to "seek other quarters." Here again, Turner chose his words carefully—only the ones who feel they are *self-reliant* should seek other quarters. Turner's use of the word "self-reliant" served two purposes. First, it addressed Turner's critics who charged that Turner wanted all African Americans to return to Africa. Turner never advocated that all blacks should return to Africa. He made this position clear in an open letter to Blanche Bruce, former U.S. senator from Mississippi in 1890.

You say, "What non-sense all this talk about sending all the blacks back to Africa is." True, you are right, if such a nefarious scheme is in contemplation, for thousand and hundreds of thousands of us are no more fit to go back to Africa than we are fit to go to Paradise. (Redkey *Respect* 76)

Second, Turner's use of the word *self-reliant* forced the audience to reflect about whether they are the ones who feel as if they were self-reliant. However, it is a false choice because of the framing of the argument in general. The self-reliant are the ones who would seek other quarters to live and the ones who do not seek other quarters are not self-reliant, and in Turner's estimation, they would not help in the overall emigration program anyway. One noticed that Turner did not give a third option here—the intention was to get his audience to choose between being *self-reliant* or not.

Turner's use of the words "seek other quarters" is interesting as well. Though known to be a supporter of *African emigration*, nowhere in the speech does Turner call explicitly for emigration to Africa. Turner invokes others' plans and proposals such as Mexican, Canadian, and South American emigration and even speaks highly of John Temple Graves' plan that would set aside a portion of land in the United States for African Americans as a "separate and distinct state" ("Negro").

Therefore, Turner's call was for a plan of action that would help relieve the suffering of African Americans. One way he advocated this position was to proclaim that America owed African Americans "billions of dollars" for slavery, making Turner one of the first to call for slavery reparations.

This nation justly, rightly, and divinely owes us work for services rendered, billions of dollars, and if we cannot be treated as American people, we should ask for five hundred million dollars, at least, to begin an emigration somewhere, for it will cost, sooner or later, far more than that amount to keep the Negro down unless they re-establish slavery itself. Freedom and perpetual degradation are not in the economy of human events. It is against reason, against nature, against precedent, and against God. ("Negro")

However, his call for reparations is conditional—reparations should only come if America cannot treat blacks as *American people*. Once again, Turner's use of language seems open to the possibility of change in America. However, from the beginning of the speech, Turner denies the possibility of change in America and therefore, references to Turner's *change* really function to induce his audience to see that there could be no change and the degradation of African Americans would continue.

Moreover, specially earmarked are reparations for emigration "somewhere." Again, Turner chooses his words carefully. He leaves the place of emigration open, and by doing so Turner invites his primarily anti-emigration audience to start thinking about emigration as a possible solution. By framing his argument this way, Turner attempts to address a major hurdle in the emigration debate. His call for reparations addresses the money issue. One major obstacle to any

emigration program is cost. Turner's solution is to challenge the government
to provide for emigration through reparations. For Turner, reparations are not
handouts or gifts, but money earned and owed for "services rendered."

Turner's reparations argument also grounds itself in what is *just, right and
divine*. Turner, as prophet, elevates the discussion of reparations and places it in
a moral sphere. By doing this, not only does he invite his audience to look at this
radical position more seriously, he also invites his audience to reflect on the
fairness of the country. Turner's aim of course is to get the audience to *see* what
he sees—that America has not been fair to African Americans therefore they
should consider emigration as a viable option and that African Americans
should receive compensation to support this emigration enterprise.

For Turner, the attitude of the nation towards African Americans was beyond repair. Therefore, his aim was to get his audience to recognize this *fact* in
order to act—because without recognition, no action would take place. While
Turner's position *did allow for change*, he just did not see it coming, and since it
would be "folly" to attempt to resist or fight, African Americans ought to seek
out other places to live.

Therefore, the hope Turner promotes is the hope to *act within one's own
moral agency* and achieve genuine *personhood*. Once African Americans see the
situation as he does, a hopeless situation turns hopeful. As Turner warns earlier
in his speech, to stay in America and to occupy an "ignoble status with the possibility of being shot, hung, or burnt" would be to declare African Americans
"unfit to be free men or to assume the responsibilities which involve fatherhood
and existence" ("Negro"). However, to do something else—to do something like
"seeking other quarters"—is the hope that Turner proclaims and he argues that it
is not too late for this action to take place.

At the end of Turner's speech, the audience erupted in applause and throughout
the speech, the audience shouted and cheered (Redkey, *Black Exodus* 187).
However, by the end of the convention, it was clear that the overwhelming majority of delegates were not in favor of emigration anywhere. Instead of an emigration plan, the only recommendations that came out of the convention were to
establish the National Equal Rights Council, with Turner acting as *chancellor*
and to continue to appeal to Congress, governors, and the American people for
fair and equal justice.

For Turner this was not enough. In an article published after the Convention
in the *Voice of Missions*, Turner sarcastically asked, "What under heaven would
[I] want with a national convention of over seven hundred delegates to endorse
African emigration, when at least two million of colored people here in the
South are ready to start to Africa at any moment, if we had a line of steamers
running to and fro" ("Turner" *VM*, Jan. 1894). Indeed, Turner had created interest in emigration, but without the funds for transportation it was just a dream on
the part of Turner and his supporters.

Frustrated by society's dealings with African Americans and annoyed by African American responses to unjust treatment, Turner began to shift from being a person who believed African Americans would fully integrate into American society, to one who argued that there was no personhood future for blacks in America. While Turner believed that American society would never give equal rights to African Americans, his radical egalitarian notions of equal rights and inclusion did not wane. In short, Turner believed in and supported the principles of America, but argued that African Americans would never have the chance to participate in those principles in America.

It was Turner's belief about America's unwillingness to live up to the covenant as it related to African Americans and not the covenant itself that posed the problem. Therefore, since Turner no longer felt a call to be a prophet for America, there was no reason for him to call America to live up or come back to its covenant. For Turner, America was in an apostate condition that only God could cure. In the meantime, African Americans should do all in their power to "seek other quarters."

However, Turner concluded that African Americans would not seek those others quarters—they would stay in America. This led Turner to shift his prophetic persona yet again. He would find strength in adversity, and as the nineteenth century came to a close Turner would increase his critique and prophetic denouncements about the church, society in general, and especially other African American leaders. Instead of becoming a nihilist or someone who escaped to "seek other quarters," Turner stayed in America, suffered the indignities along with the people who now became his base of support—the poor and destitute sharecroppers of the South. He began to chronicle and highlight their frustration, pain, and suffering. They would need someone to speak for them, because America was primed to become even more hostile toward African Americans. Moreover, African Americans were also about to get a new leader who, though friendly with Turner, would clash with him on the idea of emigration.

Notes

1. Paps Singleton led many African Americans from the South to Kansas in 1879.

2. The fact that many slave owners did not want to teach their slaves the Christian faith for fear that they may want to be free attest to Turner's claims. See H. Sheldon *Smith's In His Image, But: Racism in Southern Religion, 1790-1910.*

3. This is a common feature in prophetic rhetoric. It is the belief that God is working through evil to bring forth good. For more on this concept see Ernest G Bormann, "Fetching Good out of Evil: A Rhetorical use of Calamity," *Quarterly Journal of Speech* 63.2 (1977): 130-140.

Chapter Four

"No Future for the Negro": Turner's Pessimistic Prophecy

Once a believer that America was the messianic hope for all people, Turner shifted to a belief that true personhood status and fair treatment as human beings was not forthcoming for African Americans in America. Therefore, Turner argued that emigration would be the best answer for solving the problems that plagued African Americans.

Tricky as this rhetorical position was, Turner still offered hope that emigration could happen. However, after the Convention, Turner's hope that African Americans would emigrate to Africa began to wane. Though still convinced that emigration was the answer to the problems plaguing blacks at the time, Turner realized that too many factors were working against his emigration campaign. One of those factors was the Convention itself. In its final resolution, the Convention took emigration off the table because the majority of the delegates wanted to "see if we can make it possible to live here as citizens of the United States, and enjoy the respect, rights and privileges accorded to other people" ("Bishop Turner Tells," *The Freedman*, Jan. 13, 1894).

Therefore, once again, Turner faced a rhetorical hurdle. How could he find rhetorical space and relevance for a program that seemed unachievable, and how could Turner operate within the public sphere when he rejected programs of accommodation and assimilation as inadequate to address the myriad of problems African Americans faced? How did Turner find his voice when he believed his program—even though the best from his view—was not achievable? It was out of his deeply held emigration beliefs that Turner shifted his prophetic persona yet again, moving towards *pessimistic prophecy* and hurling invectives and prophetic laments upon his audiences and society.

93

In this chapter, I attempt to demonstrate Turner's pessimistic turn and his prophetic laments by examining his speech "The American Negro and his Fatherland," given in 1895 at the Congress on Africa. The speech—given roughly two months after Booker T. Washington's *Atlanta Compromise* speech—is important for study because it not only demonstrates some of the differences between the two, it also is an example of another type of resistance strategy employed by blacks as they navigated the maze of racism and oppression.

Even though there was never a complete halt to emigration schemes and campaigns throughout the rest of the nineteenth and early twentieth centuries, most African Americans accepted that African emigration was not going to become a reality. The more prosperous blacks in the North did not think African emigration was feasible or prudent and the less prosperous blacks in the South could not afford to emigrate. Therefore, African Americans began to look elsewhere for answers to the problems they faced from society.

In the North, black leaders continued to push for integration at all levels— promoting ideas of equal rights and equal opportunity. However, as the plight of Southern blacks continued to deteriorate, black leaders in the North begin also to push for equal protection of life, liberty, and property (Condit and Lucaites 139). One example of this was the speech given by Fredrick Douglass at the Metropolitan AME church in Washington, D.C. on January 9, 1894. Entitled "Lessons for the Hour," the speech not only calls for equal rights, opportunity, and protection for African Americans, but it also offers a stinging critique of emigration.

Douglass called emigration part of the family of "low bred ideas" and said that it was "nonsense to talk about the removal of eight millions of the American people from their homes in America to Africa" (24). In a direct attack at Turner, Douglass says about emigration, "The bad thing about it is that it now has begun to be advocated by colored men of acknowledged ability and learning" and "my opinion of them is that if they are sensible, they are insincere, and if they are sincere they are not sensible" (25). Douglass felt that it would not only be foolish of the government to spend millions of dollars to send African Americans to Africa but it also offered no hope to African Americans in their progress as an "American citizen." Douglass stated about emigration:

> It tends to weaken his hold on one country while it can give him no rational hope of another. Its tendency is to make him despondent and doubtful, where he should be made to feel assured and confident. It forces upon him the idea that he is forever doomed to be a stranger and sojourner in the land of his birth, and that he has no permanent abiding place here. All of this is hurtful, with such ideas constantly flaunted before him he cannot easily set himself to work to better his condition in such ways as are open to him here. It sets him to groping everlasting after the impossible. (26)

In closing, Douglass acknowledged that emigration was not the answer to the so-called Negro Problem. He also did not offer any concrete answers or solutions outside of charging the white people of the North and South to "conquer their prejudices," and challenging America to stop "violating the amendments of the Constitution of the United States, and no longer evading the claims of justice" (33).

However, a more practical and pragmatic response would come from the South in the form of Booker T. Washington—founder and principal of Tuskegee Institute in Tuskegee, Alabama. While he quietly built a reputation by promoting what Mixon calls the "Hampton Idea" (367) for his school, Washington came to the attention of mainstream society on September 18, 1895 with his *Atlanta Exposition* address. Commonly called the *Atlanta Compromise*, Washington offered a new program for African Americans grounded in friendship between whites and blacks and compromise.

Washington began his speech by invoking praise of the leaders of the Exposition for "generously recognizing" the "value and manhood of the American Negro" and this effort would "do more to cement the friendship of the two races than any occurrence since the dawn of freedom" (6). He believed the Exposition would awaken in African Americans a "new era of industrial progress" because heretofore African Americans, because of "ignorance and inexperience," had sought after life "at the top" instead of at the bottom (6).

Therefore, Washington called for blacks to "cast down your buckets where you are" and make "friends in every manly way of the people of all races by whom we are surrounded" (7). He also called for whites to do the same and reject "those of foreign birth and strange tongue" and "cast it down" among African Americans "whose habits you know, and "whose fidelity and love you have tested" (8). In a swipe at Turner, Washington criticized not only emigration schemes, but also "social equality" as "folly" opting to be "separate as the fingers, yet one as the hand in all things essential to mutual progress" (9-11).

Washington's speech catapulted him into the national spotlight with the mantle of being the new *Negro Leader*. He seemed to be the answer for both blacks and whites. First, he offered for blacks another answer to the failed promises of emigration campaigns and slow integration possibilities. For whites, he offered a reprieve from black leaders demanding political and social equality. Washington's nationalistic program of *accommodation* led many blacks to believe equality would come if only they were *subservient enough* and knew their places in society.

While Washington's program of accommodation catapulted him to national status, Turner continued to focus on emigration as the solution to the problems besieging African Americans. Turner maintained a heavy speaking schedule in part because of his status as one of the bishops of the AME Church, turned his attention primarily to his duties as editor of the *Voice of Missions*, and wrote many editorials defining his position on emigration and commenting on others who disagreed with him.[1]

Turner did not only limit himself to his own newspaper. He was also a frequent guest editorialist at other well-known daily newspapers. For instance, he began the year 1895 writing an open letter to African Americans published in

the *Atlanta Constitution* titled, "To the Colored People of the United States."
In this letter, Turner expressed that he wanted African Americans to take part in
the Cotton States and International Exposition that local leadership would hold
later that year.[2]

However, it was not long before he promoted emigration as the ultimate solution to the problems African American faced.

> I believe that two or three millions of us ought to go to Africa and build up a
> civilized nation and show the world that we can be statesmen, generals, bank-
> ers, merchants, philosophers, inventors and everything that anybody else is. I
> further believe that if a half-million of us would ask congress for an appropria-
> tion to assist us to return to the land of our ancestry so that we might increase
> the commerce of this nation and begin the civilization of Africa, as God in-
> tended for us to do, we would get it, but because I have dared to write and
> speak my sentiments, I am denounced by this do-nothing party in unmeasured
> terms. The same men who are fighting the exposition are fighting African emi-
> gration. ("To Colored People")

Later that year in December, Turner accepted an invitation to present a paper at the Congress on Africa as part of the Exposition sponsored by Gammon
Theological Seminary in December of 1895.[3] The Congress convened at the
Colored Methodist Church in Atlanta. Leaders invited people to deliver papers
on the political, spiritual, and economic condition of Africa. The papers, gathered by John Wesley Edward Bowen, professor of historical theology at Gammon and published as a book entitled *Africa and the American Negro*, served to
promote interest in African missionary work and not necessarily emigration.

Though Turner at this time began to doubt whether African Americans
would ever emigrate to Africa, the renewed interest in Africa as a *missionary
field* created excitement for him. The basic premise was that Africans were in
need of civilization and that Christianity would be the best vehicle to "civilize
the heathen." It was also during this time that several denominations began to set
up missionary aid societies to spread the gospel to Africa.

Turner, along with other luminaries of the time, was to speak on the theme:
The American Negro: His Relation to the Civilization and Redemption of Africa.
Inherent in the theme was a discussion on African Americans and their role in
helping civilize and redeem Africa. While other speakers on Turner's panel
spoke of a glorious future for African Americans in spite of the hardships they
faced, Turner took a different approach—he used his presentation at the conference to drive home much larger themes affecting African Americans in America.

The American Negro and the Fatherland

In his opening remarks, Turner asserted that it would be a "waste of time" to
"expend much labor" in discussing the present status of the "Negroid race in the

United States" since it is "too well known already" (Turner, "American" 195).
Turner's remarks led the audience to believe, at least early on in the speech, that
he would not address problems facing African Americans nor offer any critiques
of people or institutions he believed hindered progress for blacks. His assertion
that "it is too well known already" assumed his audience was aware of this and
no further attention given to the pain and frustration of blacks would do any
good.

Turner strengthened this assumption when he immediately revisited an old
theme first articulated in his *Emancipation Day* speech in 1866—his view on
slavery. Turner still argued that slavery "was brought to this country in the providence of God to a heaven-permitted if not divine-sanctioned manual laboring
school" so that the African would "have direct contact with the mightiest race
that ever trod the face of the earth" ("American" 195).[4]

By the time of his "American Negro and his Fatherland" speech, Turner's
views about slavery began to change. While always believing that God allowed
slavery *under the providential covering of God,* Turner, drawing from the work
of black historian George Washington Williams, challenged long-held conceptions that Africans came to America by the "avarice of the white man, single and
alone." Turner now argued the "white slave purchaser" went to Africa and
bought "our ancestors from their African masters" and those first slaves were
actually the children of slaves in Africa who had been slaves for "a thousand
years" ("American" 195).[5] Therefore, Turner reasoned, the argument that the
"white man went to African and stole us, [was] not true."

> They brought us out of slavery that still exists over a large portion of that con-
> tinent. For there are millions and millions of slaves in Africa today. Thus the
> superior African sent us and the white man brought us, and we remained in
> slavery as long as it was necessary to learn that a God, who is spirit, made the
> world and controls it, and that Supreme Being could be sought and found by
> the exercise of faith in His only begotten Son. (195)

When slavery ended, African Americans were "thrown upon [their] own responsibility" and therefore they stand in the "providence of God" a free people able
to make their own decisions ("American" 195).

As he did in his "Emancipation Day" speech, Turner appropriated a pro-
slavery argument—that slavery was a good thing because slaves learned Christianity. However, the appropriation of this pro-slavery argument, while allowing
Turner the rhetorical space to pursue another avenue of interpretation, was vast-
ly different from his 1866 speech. In his Emancipation speech, Turner argued
that slavery was *a trust from God* and it was the responsibility of whites to
teach, train, and provide for the enslaved. Moreover, the reason slavery failed
was because whites failed to live up to the trust. However, by 1895, Turner's
position changed. In this speech, Turner argued that whites apparently *did live
up to their charge* because enslaved Africans *did learn* about God and Christianity, and only remained in slavery "as long as it was necessary" to learn the faith.

Therefore, slavery ended when whites finished their job—teaching enslaved Africans Christianity.

While Turner's position and beliefs about slavery changed primarily because of Williams' thesis, one cannot discount Turner's rhetorical application to this new position. The shift comes at a time when Turner had already begun to change his prophetic persona. One of Turner's frustrations was his belief blacks were not doing anything to help their own situation. By offering this *new* interpretation of slavery, Turner positioned African Americans as a people who could claim their own agency because slavery only "went down" because God in God's providence knew that African Americans were ready to stand on their "own responsibility" and "cultivate" a sense of "self-reliance and imbibing a knowledge of civil law" ("American" 195).

Therefore, to support his position, Turner argued that African Americans had been "free" long enough to begin to think for themselves and begin "planning for better conditions outside of the United States" ("American" 195). Turner, as he mentioned in his "Negro Convention" speech, believed there was no "manhood future" for blacks in America. Turner argued that African Americans "may eke out an existence for generations to come, but he could never be a man—full, symmetrical and undwarfed."

While Turner argued African Americans can claim agency and make decisions because they are now free to do so, he at the same time limited those decisions. The only valid decision in Turner's estimation was "planning for better conditions outside the United States" because in America, African Americans could never enjoy full personhood. Therefore, African Americans are limited to a freedom that means only "eking out an existence" instead of living life to its fullest. Turner's answer to this dilemma was of course emigration, but by 1895, he knew that this was not the answer preferred by most African Americans. So, how did he create the rhetorical space to promote his agenda while many other voices were speaking accommodation and/or assimilation? I suggest that Turner adopted a prophetic persona as a pessimistic prophet believing America will not change, thereby leaving emigration to Africa as the only viable option.

"There is No Manhood Status for the Negro"

Turner believed there would never be any personhood (manhood) status for African Americans in America. In an earlier editorial written in the *Voice of Missions*, Turner defined manhood as the opportunity to "achieve distinction and honor" because without that "no people or race can progress and develop the mighty powers that lie dormant in them" (Turner, "Home" March 1895). For Turner, as long as the opportunity to achieve "distinction and honor" was not afforded to African Americans, they would always be a group of "menials" and "scullions"—a subservient group of people not worthy of respect from others or each other ("Home").

While acknowledging that those "who make pretensions to scholarship," both "white and colored," will not only differ from him but also charge him with "folly," Turner nevertheless would "itemize and give a cursory glance at a few facts calculated to convince any man who is not biased or lamentable ignorant" about this subject ("American" 195). By framing his argument this way, Turner accomplished two things. First, Turner's aim here was not to convince his opponents of the necessity of emigration, but to convince them of his vision—that he saw no personhood future for African Americans in America. Second, by recognizing his opponents and constructing his argument this way, Turner positioned himself as the one attacked. By adopting a persona of a lone prophet crying in the wilderness, Turner positioned himself as the only one who saw that African Americans did not have any real future in America. Therefore, his *prophetic wail* grounded itself in the hope that after sharing the real situation with others, especially his opponents, they too will come around to see what he saw.

Turner further developed his prophetic persona when he limited the understanding and scope of his vision. The vision was not granted to the "biased" or the "ignorant" because, in Turner's estimation, they cannot be convinced anyway. True to prophetic practices, not everyone hearing the vision will receive it; therefore, the prophet is not under any illusions that *all will hear and receive*. Nevertheless, Turner addressed his audience knowing that perhaps only a few would *see what he saw*.

First, Turner saw a great chasm between black and white. While he saw this chasm all over the world, he aimed his criticisms at America. Turner blamed this chasm on white people who will not have any *social contact* between themselves and "any portion of the Negroid race" ("American" 196). Turner suggested the reason for this is the belief that "one drop of African blood imparts a taint." This is also why Turner argued that the talk about the two races "remaining in the same country with mutual interest and responsibility" and no social contact is the "jargon of folly." To support his argument he quoted segregationist senator John Tyler Morgan of Alabama when he says, "The negro has nothing to expect without social equality with the whites and the whites will never grant it" ("American" 196).

Turner argued that leaders who would engage in "scholarship," which he defined as "wading through dusty volumes for forty and fifty years," instead of reading "trashy articles of newspapers," would not "dare to predict symmetrical manhood for the Negroid race in this or any other country, without social equality" ("American" 196). Turner also took a swipe at Booker T. Washington and other accommodationists who did not want social equality. Turner argued that the person "who will in one breath say African Americans do not want social equality" and in the next breath predict great things from the race is either "an ignoramus or is an advocate of the perpetual servility and degradation of his race variety" ("American" 196).

However, while blaming whites for not allowing social equality, Turner suggested maybe God did not want whites to offer social equality in America.

By claiming a divine predisposition behind the separation of the races, Turner argued for the emigration of "two or three million of us to return to the land of our ancestors and establish our own nation" to not only "give the world the benefit of our individuality but to build up social conditions peculiarly our own" ("American" 196). Turner saw America as a "white man's country" or the "country he claims and is bound to dominate" and sees no other alternative for an equal "civil status" for African Americans thereby giving fuel to his emigration proposals.

The "civil status" of African Americans came at the mercy and "free will" of whites and left African Americans able to "demand nothing." Turner reminded his audience that blacks were deposed from juries and "tried and convicted by men who do not claim to be his peers" and treated unjustly on the railways where African Americans "must ride the Jim Crow car or walk" ("American" 196). In addition, he recalled the Supreme Court decision that declared the 1875 Civil Rights Bill unconstitutional. For Turner, this was more than just a decision—it was a license that declared the "colored man had no civil rights under the general government," that allowed "several states to limit, curtail and deprive" African Americans these rights and privileges and "disfranchise" blacks.

Secondly, Turner argued that conditions in America were so bad that African Americans suffered from an inferiority complex. While conceding that the discrimination laws were degrading to both the victim and degrader, Turner focused on African Americans. Turner argued "degradation begets degradation," and therefore "any people oppressed, proscribed, belied, slandered, burned, flayed and lynched" will not only become "cowardly and servile," but they will pass this "servility on to their posterity and will continue to do so *ad infinitum*" and will "never make a bold and courageous people" ("American" 197, emphasis original).

For Turner, since the condition of African Americans was so "repugnant," many blacks passed for whites because they did not want to "be black because of its ignoble condition," but since they cannot be white, they "unrace" themselves and become "monstrosities" ("American" 197). Turner, anticipating arguments made by Carter G. Woodson almost forty years later, argued that blacks who are "educated by white teachers never have any respect for people their own color and spend their days as devotees of white gods" ("American" 197).[6]

In addition, Turner argued that the language the "white man" used was also degrading to black people. Foreshadowing Malcolm X and other Black Nationalist orators in the twentieth century, Turner noted everything "satanic, corrupt, and infamous is denominated black," and everything constituting "virtue, purity, innocence, religion" and all that is "divine and heavenly is represented as white ("American" 197). Turner lamented "Sabbath school teaching" because church leaders unknowingly taught to sing to the laudation of white and the contempt of black. This led him to ask rhetorically, "Can anyone with an ounce of common sense expect that these children, when they reach maturity, will ever have any respect for their black or colored faces, or the faces of their associates" (197). Therefore, since in America, "white represents God and black represents the devil," the African American should "build up a nation" and "create a language in keeping with his color as the whites have done" because African Americans will never respect themselves until they do (197).

Thirdly, in disavowing social equality, Turner argued that African Americans could not use their own faculties and genius to contribute something to society. Turner argued that African Americans wait for whites to "propose, project, erect, invent, discover, combine, plan and execute everything connected with civilization" and doing this "dwarfs the colored man and allows his great faculties to slumber from the cradle to the grave" (197-198).

Turner further argues that African Americans possessed "mechanical and inventive genius equal to any race on earth (198). For proof, Turner recalled the days "before the war" when African Americans "erected and completed all of the fine edifices in which the lords of the land luxuriated" (198). Although whites talked about the "natural inability" of blacks, Turner called it "idle talk" and suggested that blacks need a "country and surroundings in harmony with his color and with respect for his manhood" (198).

Turner explained that he could continue this line of thought if he had time but then quickly acknowledged the "thousands of people" who advise the "colored people to stay out of politics," but yet "do not advise themselves" (198). Turner reasoned, "if the Negro is a man in keeping with other men, why should he be less concerned about politics than any one else?" (198) He then took aim again at Washington and other "would-be colored leaders" who promote the idea that African Americans should not concern themselves with politics. Turner argued that the argument that they should "stay out of politics" was to reduce them to the level of a "horse or a cow," and the "negro who does it proclaims his inability to take part in political affairs (198). Therefore, for Turner, "if the Negro is to be a man, full and complete, he must take part in everything that belongs to manhood," and if "he omits a single duty, responsibility or privilege, to that extent he is limited and incomplete" (198).

After apologizing because time had not allowed him to discuss this topic further, Turner concluded his speech with an answer to his critics who called his emigration position an "advertisement of folly" (198). Turner believed two hundred and fifty million dollars would be enough to "rid this country of the last member of the Negroid race" and the general government could "furnish this without ever missing it." Turner also reasoned this amount would "only be the pitiful sum of a million dollars a year" for the time African Americans "labored for nothing and which somebody or some power is responsible" (198). After mentioning the estimated millions of immigrants who come to America every year with "no public stir about it," Turner ended the speech suggesting that only two or three million "self reliant men and women" go to Africa and establish the conditions in which he advocated (198).

Turner's Pessimistic Vision

To understand Turner's pessimism, we have to understand why Turner believed that whites would never favor nor grant *social equality* to blacks and how blacks adopted its use and at least rhetorically, supported their own oppression. After slavery and leading up to this period, many black leaders frequently denied they wanted *social equality*. While reasons varied, many blacks adopted the *Southern whites'* definition of equality. Condit and Lucaites in their book *Crafting Equality* noted one reason that blacks rejected social equality was that the term had come to function as a code word for "interracial marriage and racial amalgamation" (123). Black leaders were quick to remind whites they had no desire for interracial marriage or race mixing.

Yet still another reason for disavowing social equality was that blacks, especially middle and upper-middle class blacks, while disapproving of discrimination based solely on race, did approve *discrimination on an individual basis*. In other words, some blacks believed that social equality would force them to associate with whites who did not measure up to the standards of some middle class blacks. They felt, along with Southern whites, that the government could not "control the respect" or "compel personal intimacy" between people who did not want to be together (Condit and Lucaites 107).

While one can argue that blacks' disavowal of social equality might be a case of strategic essentialism, this strategy also set up a rhetorical problem. As Condit and Lucaites note:

> If they agreed to a federal ban on Social Equality, they implicitly acknowledged their inferiority in a system that placed being white at the top of the hierarchy, an implication that white supremacists in particular would quickly seize. If they challenged such a proscription, they would be interpreted as aspiring to the top of the hierarchy. (123)

However, Turner defined social equality differently. While other black leaders separated social equality from all other types of equality, in an earlier response to Booker T. Washington's *Atlanta Compromise* speech published in the *Voice of Missions*, Turner maintained that the term social equality itself carried with it "civil, political, financial, judicial, and business equality" (Redkey, *Respect* 166). In short, Turner saw social equality as the basis for true equality and without it the "sequel must be discrimination, proscription, injustice, and degradation" (Redkey, *Respect* 166). Turner further argued that Washington and others who denied social equality gave license to whites to argue that the "Negro race is satisfied with being degraded" and that they would have to live a long time to "undo the harm [they have] done to our race" (Redkey, *Respect* 166). Therefore, for Turner, blacks who disavowed social equality but predicted a glorious future for African Americans were "ignorant" because by denying social equality they were promoting the "perpetual servility and degradation of [the] race variety" ("American" 198).

Also, without social equality, the "civil status" of blacks was contingent upon whites. Without any agency on their own, blacks could "demand nothing." States could enact laws that "limit, curtail, and deprive" blacks of "civil rights, immunities, and privileges" and would lead to perpetual disfranchisement. In other words, their disavowing of social equality hampered black leaders fighting for and demanding civil and political equality. For Turner, African Americans were not going to get any type of equality without first getting social equality.

Moreover, the degradation caused by social inequality, in Turner's view, would pass to later generations. Thus, an unintended consequence of not having social equality with whites would be to produce a people who would become "cowardly and servile" and who could never become "bold and courageous." This produced a problem in Turner's estimation because it made the conditions of African Americans so bad that an inherent lack of "self-respect" developed. Turner found examples of problems of identity and personhood when blacks passed for white and when black teachers did not respect or believe in their black students. Without social equality, identity and personhood could not develop because self-respect hinged on one's own belief in oneself as a person. By denying social equality, blacks inherently denied themselves the self-respect needed to operate within a world that separated them not only by status but, as Turner noted, by language as well.

As a solution to the plight of African Americans, Turner advocated emigration to Africa. However, by 1895, Turner knew he was in a distinct minority. Others who earlier advocated African emigration, most notably Alexander Crummell, had distanced themselves from an emigration position in favor of promoting a vision of hard work and race development that eventually would lead to integration.[7]

Turner, on the other hand, saw America differently. Turner did not see whites and blacks together because whites would never grant social equality. He believed that social equality was the "pivotal point of every form of respectability" (Redkey, *Respect* 162) and without it, there would never be any true equality of any kind. Therefore, the American Creed did not apply to blacks, not because the creed was not applicable to blacks, but because the holders and shapers of the creed would not allow African Americans to participate. Participation in the creed came only by social interaction with others who also participated in the creed. Therefore, a separate location within the same nation and dependent upon the same structures to support the same groups of separated people could never work. The stronger or the one that assumed the top of the hierarchal structure would always dominate and eventually destroy the other. Thus, Turner's vision was pessimistic because he did not believe whites were ever going to grant social equality.

Turner's Prophetic Lament

While Turner adopted a prophetic persona that was pessimistic, a closer look at
his rhetoric reveals that Turner's pessimism was not derived from a fundamental
belief that America's covenant was wrong or bad—Turner never called for
America to adopt another covenant, nor did he ever directly challenge America's
creed. Turner's pessimism derived from a foundational belief that America
would not include African Americans within the covenant. In other words, the
notions of freedom, justice, civilization, equality, and all the other words associated with America were bedrock values, and Turner appreciated them—he just
did not believe America was ready to share those same values with African
Americans.

Therefore, since America would not allow African Americans to participate
in the covenant, there was no need to call America to live up to the covenant as
in the jeremiad. America, Turner believed, had already decided against extending the covenant to include African Americans. In addition, while Turner
thought America was headed for another war or some major catastrophe that
would do major damage to the country, he did not become an apocalyptic
prophet because he did not believe God would bring forth a new day when
blacks and whites would work together. In short, Turner believed nothing would
change.

Turner also believed that blacks would never become a people who would
experience a divine call to go to Africa. He began to see that the majority of
African Americans who could have afforded to go to Africa did not want to go
and the ones who wanted to go could not afford to go. Though he continued to
regard Africa as the "fatherland" for blacks and to believe that African Americans could build a great nation there, he eventually came to see that his plan was
not realistic.

The problems African Americans faced were real and the solutions offered
did not seem to alleviate the sufferings and injustices African Americans experienced on a daily basis. For Turner, the northern African American response of
assimilation/integration embodied in the rhetoric of Fredrick Douglass, and
eventually W.E.B. DuBois, did not help because of white resistance in both the
North and South. The Southern African American response of accommodation
represented in the rhetoric of Booker T. Washington did not help because it not
only placed African Americans in subordinate positions, but also in so doing,
stamped blacks with a badge of inferiority, which damaged African American
identity and self-image.

Turner argued that he had a concrete and pragmatic plan that would address
the weaknesses of both responses. Emigration would negate white indifference
to integration and, at the same time, offer African Americans a chance to build
self-esteem and self-worth by creating institutions and systems supportive and
respectful of their personhood. However, Turner's emigration proposal had its

own flaws and he eventually came to the position that African Americans were not going to emigrate to Africa nor any place else.

Therefore, Turner finds himself in a rhetorical abyss. Since Turner could not draw upon the jeremiad or apocalyptic prophecies, and could not draw upon previous prophecies as he had done in the past, how could he still adopt a prophetic persona and find voice within this rhetorical space? Turner positioned himself within the *lament tradition of prophecy*. Since America would not live up to its covenant and since Turner did not feel America was in for an apocalyptic doomsday, these avenues of prophetic discourse were not available. Thus, Turner offered laments and became a *wailing and moaning prophet* whose primary function was to speak out on the behalf of others and to chronicle their pain and suffering as well as his own.

The lament tradition has a long and rich history in biblical studies and does not warrant full treatment here.[8] As noted earlier, a lament is a woeful complaint done primarily in private by an individual that highlights issues and problems that a person or group faces. Usually this complaint is directly addressed to God in prayer and loaded with rhetorical questions of "why." "Why am I going through this," "why am I still feeling all alone," and "why is this happening to me" are standard laments when individuals are feeling the burden of explaining the unexplainable.

Turner's lamentations, however, are different. First, Turner's lamentations are not private but public and second, instead of directly addressing God, Turner's lamentations address the public. Therefore, Turner practices a *public lamentation* that invites all who hear (or read) his words to understand his frustration and pain but also to know and to understand something about the pain and frustration of the people he claims to represent. Barbara Holmes suggests that public laments "wake us up" and they require a "shift from the individual whine to the corporate moan, from personal annoyance to collective angst, from egocentric agenda to the spirit and intent of the community" (36).

Consistent with the lament tradition, Turner does not expect anything to change—racism, lynching, and all the other problems African Americans faced would continue. His goal is simply *to speak and to get his audience to hear*. Thus, Turner's prophecy becomes a record chronicling the pains and sufferings of the people he claims to represent and giving voice to the voiceless.

Turner's lament, as part of the *sharing of the real situation* in prophetic discourse, is all the more relevant to study because it differs from much of African American rhetoric during this period. Regardless of whether it was an assimilationist/integrationist response or one of accommodation, these responses had embedded within them one similar feature—*a hope for a bright and glorious future for blacks in America*. This bright future found resonance in the oft-promoted successes gained by blacks since Emancipation—successes that included property ownership, educational achievements, number of businesses opened and maintained, and the religious advancement of African Americans.[9] This is not to say that African American assimilationist/integrationist and accommodationist leaders did not mention the struggles and suffering that took place within the African American community—it just was not the focus of much of their rhetoric.

Turner, on the other hand, not only highlighted the pain and suffering of African Americans, but also made it the focus of his rhetoric. This *focus* fit within the lament tradition of prophecy—a tradition that could house Turner's bitterness and anger with both the system that would not allow blacks to take part and with what he believed to be the apathetic nature of many black leaders. At the same time, it gave Turner a voice as a pessimistic prophetic who declared, "There is no manhood future in the United States for the Negro."

However, where is the hope in *prophetic pessimism* if it is indeed a type of prophetic discourse? I argue that there is hope in prophetic pessimism because it grounds itself within the *public lament tradition of prophecy*, which focuses primarily on a heightened awareness of the *real situation*, the naming of the *ills* or *demons* of society with the *hope in being heard*. It is a hope that finds its residence exclusively within the community that the prophet claims to represent.

To this end, we must now ask what community Turner represented in the speech. As I noted in chapter 2, after his "Eligibility" speech Turner's prophetic persona shifted from a universal prophet—one who called for both blacks and whites to work together under the sacredness of the American covenant—to one who primarily represented the African American community. Whether he invoked God's judgment and vindication as he did in his "Eligibility" speech, or charged his audience to take pride in themselves, or challenged them to see themselves in a different light, Turner's hope found its home in the black community. However, as Turner's prophetic persona began to shift yet again, he no longer represented the *entire black community*—he represented only *Southern blacks*, who were for the most part feeling the pains of racism and Jim Crow legislation more than Northern blacks were.

In addition, Turner's prophetic pessimism allowed him to become more philosophical and allowed for a deep and more penetrating analysis of current situations facing African Americans. In this speech we get a glimpse of what would become a staple for Turner throughout the rest of his life—a sharpened focus on black identity and self-respect. Though many scholars recognize DuBois as the *father of black identity studies* because of his oft-cited "double consciousness" phrase, Turner first saw how a flawed construction of identity would be detrimental to African Americans. Grounded in his prophetic pessimism, Turner saw what social scientists and cultural critics would later acknowledge in the twentieth century—that segregation had an injurious effect upon African Americans.

In this chapter, I suggest that Turner shifted from an optimistic to pessimistic prophet. While Turner's pessimism began much earlier, he believed African Americans, when given correct information about Africa, would strive to constitute a new identity and accept the call of emigration. However, with Northern integrationist rhetoric strong and with the rise of Booker T. Washington and the rhetoric of accommodation, Turner began to doubt emigration would ever take place. Therefore, Turner became a prophetic pessimist whose rhetoric found a home within the lament tradition of prophecy. It was within the lament tradition that Turner could still find relevance as an orator by not only offering critiques of society but also offering critiques of black leadership that Turner felt was not relevant to the needs of the poorer Southern blacks he represented.

Turner's pessimism continued throughout the rest of his life. As Turner's pessimism grew, he also became bitter and more forceful in his attacks against society and against other African Americans who still found hope in anti-emigration policies such as integration and accommodation. Just five months after his "Fatherland" speech, Turner pessimism seemed vindicated because on May 18, 1896, the Supreme Court *officially* ruled that "separate but equal" was the law of the land. While other black leaders called for patience and tried to find some good in the decision, Turner blasted it in an editorial in the *Voice and Mission* under a headline that read, "Sackcloth and Ashes for the Negro." For Turner, it was his prophecy coming true—now states had the right under the law to segregate, and social equality was not achievable and could not become a reality. African Americans would always lack equality in every sphere of society.

Notes

1. Turner was editor of the *Voice of Missions* from Jan. 1893-Dec. 1900.

2. Many African American did not want to support the Exposition because of Jim Crow laws in the South. Booker T. Washington addressed the audience at this same Exposition.

3. For a more detailed review of the Congress, see Elliott P. Skinner, *African American and U.S. Policy Toward Africa, 1850-1924: In Defense of Black Nationality* (Washington, D.C.: Howard University Press, 1992).

4. Not every black leader agreed with Turner on his views of slavery. For a contrasting view see J.E.W. Bowen, "The Comparative Status of the Negro at the Close of the War and of To-day," in *Africa and the American Negro* (Atlanta: Gammon Theological Seminary, 1895).

5. Williams not only argued that the Africans brought to America during the middle passage were slaves of royal Africans, but these slaves were also drawn primarily from the criminal and refuse classes of African society. In short, the slaves in America came from the worst of the worst. Turner would draw more heavily on this line of thinking as his prophetic rhetoric became more and more pessimistic as racism and inequality continued to go unabated, offering this as an excuse why African Americans did not want to emigrate to Africa. See George Washington Williams, *History of the Negro Race in America: From 1619-1880*, vol. II (New York: Putnum and Sons, 1883).

6. See Carter G. Woodson, *The Miseducation of the Negro* (Associate Publishers, 1933).

7. To read Turner's analysis of Crummell's changed position, see "Home of the Blacks" in the *Voice of Mission*, March 1895.

8. For more information on the lament tradition, see Tyron Inbody, *The Transforming God: An Interpretation of Suffering and Evil* (Louisville: Westminster John Knox Press, 1997); Sally Brown, *Lament: Reclaiming Practices in the Pulpit, Pew and Public Square* (Louisville: Westminster John Knox Press, 2005); Samuel Balentine, *Prayer in the Hebrew Bible: The Drama of the Divine-Human Dialogue* (Minneapolis: Fortress Press, 1993).

9. See Alexander Crummell's "A Defense of the Negro Race in America."

Conclusion

For the remainder of his life, Turner found himself out of the mainstream of both American and African American political and social thought. His prophetic rhetoric became more and more pessimistic as black oppression and racism went unabated. However, as I mentioned in the last chapter, this pessimistic prophetic rhetoric reflected the lament tradition of prophecy. Therefore, Turner's rhetoric was both scathing and sorrowful as he cried out against injustices ranging from America's expansionist policies to America's lack of commitment to the protection of African Americans. Turner argued that emigration was the answer for disenchanted blacks, but he also knew that emigration was not a viable option because the ones who would have gone to Africa did not have the means and the ones with the means did not want to go.

However, that did not stop Turner from speaking and writing. In June of 1896, his *Voice of Missions* newspaper carried the headline "Sackcloth and Ashes for the Negro," in response to the Supreme Court's infamous Plessy v Ferguson decision (June 1, 1896). Turner's disdain for the Supreme Court went back to its 1883 decision that rendered the 1875 Civil Rights bill unconstitutional. For the rest of his life, Turner lashed out at the Supreme Court and its rulings that, in Turner's estimation, thwarted African American citizenship rights.

Because of the decision, Turner called the Supreme Court "brutal," suggested that the United States was an "organized mob" and declared he had no interest in "this bloody, lynching nation" ("Bishop Turner's Wail" July 18,1896). In response to the lynching of John Johnson and Archibald Jointly of Louisiana, the *New York Times* reported that Turner called for African Americans to defend themselves against lynch mobs. He suggested that African Americans buy guns and "keep them loaded and ready for immediate use." Turner claimed he had felt this way for "over seven years" but feared his declaration would not meet the approval of the other Bishops. However, by 1897,

Turner threw caution to the wind and declared, "Get guns Negroes, get guns, and may God give you good aim when you shoot" (March 17, 1897).[1]

In an editorial entitled "Lazy Preachers a Curse," Turner opined that the AME Church ought to purchase a huge farm and require itinerant ministers to work there for three years to "ascertain if they are lazy or not." He critiqued ministers he believed that were too lazy to have a garden, to "put away" copies of the *Christian Recorder* for their children's children, or "to chop wood, seal cracks in the floor, or to devote time to study" (*Voice of Missions*, August 1899).

Turner also took criticism for his stance on women preachers. In 1885, Turner ordained the first woman, Sarah Hughes, as an elder in the church only to have the other bishops rescind the ordination. However, that did not stop Turner from lecturing his fellow bishops and ministers about the role of women in the church. In responding to a letter he received about a male pastor complaining that the women of the church he served were getting "too fresh" and that the missionary society had "too much devilment" associated with it, Turner criticized the pastor. "The church which has an ignorant and stupid ass as that for a pastor," Turner wrote, "would be better off if they would employ a dog to bark during the church service" Further, he wrote that being opposed to "Missionary Societies is to join hands with the devil and fight God to His face" ("Is the Negro a Fool").

His criticisms also found their way toward the United States government for its escalation in Cuba and the Philippines. As a former military officer in the army and one who saw the horrors of war, Turner spoke from an enlightened position. However, his main thrust was against African Americans who fought in the wars. He argued that African Americans were fools to enlist in the Armed Forces to fight for and defend a country that would not fight and defend their rights. Turner wrote:

> If it is a white man's government, and we grant it is, let him take care of it. The Negro has no flag to defend. There is not a star in the flag of this nation, out of the forty odd, that the colored race can claim, nor is there any symbol signalized in the colors of the flag that he can presume to call his . . . unless it would be the stripes. ("The Negro," May 1899)

Turner also supported the Democratic nominee for the 1900 presidential election, William Jennings Bryan. His support was more of a protest against the Republican Party and what he believed was the abandonment of being the party of Civil Rights. He conceded that under McKinley's administration officials gave office positions to African Americans, but that did not stop the "mob violence, lynching, and burning" and that the African American "officeholders and those seeking positions are not concern about it" ("We Are For Bryan," July 1900). When the voters decided to re-elect the republican candidate McKinley over Bryan, Turner wrote a terse editorial in the *Voice of Missions* titled "McKinley, the God of Fool Negroes, Re-Elected."

However, what caused the biggest trouble for Turner was his denuncia-
tion of the flag. Turner's constant attacks against the United States and its han-
dling of lynching finally reached a crescendo when he called the flag a dirty rag.
In a speech in Macon, Georgia, the *New York Times* and other newspapers reported that Turner declared the American flag as a "dirty and contemptible rag."
Further, they reported that Turner said that "Hell was an improvement on the
United States when the Negro was involved" (*New York Times*, Feb 6, 1906).
Turner faced strong criticism after these reports and there was even talk of
bringing charges of treason against the Bishop.

In his defense, Turner suggested that he was misquoted. Turner claimed that
he did not call the flag a "dirty and contemptible rag." However, he did say,
"there was not a star in the flag that the Negro could claim or that recognized his
civil liberty and unconditional manhood, more than if it was a dirty rag." Moreover, "I did say there was more color babble in the United States than in Hell
itself: that color was unknown there" (*Philadelphia Record*, February 26, 1906).

However, the controversy did not slow Turner. In a speech in 1907 in New
York City, Turner lamented, "I used to love the American flag once myself.
Now I despise it, because America is the most horrible color-prejudice nation on
the earth. Here Negroes can be lynched, burned alive and skinned and nothing is
done about it" (*New York Times*, June 30, 1907).

That same year, Turner was married for the fourth time to Laura Lemon.
This caused consternation on the part of the other bishops because the bishops
believed that Lemon was a divorcee and it would not be prudent for one of the
bishops of the AME Church to marry such a woman. Turner defied the bishops
and married Lemon on December 3, 1907. However, as Turner biographer Stephen Angell argued, "Turner's power as bishop was severely circumscribed." At
the 1908 General Conference, there was talk about stripping Turner of his Episcopal status for his marriage to Lemon. While that did not happen, the bishops
made sure not to reappoint Turner to a district for supervision. They also had
him step down as chancellor of Morris Brown College, effectively retiring him
from his duties. Though they appointed him historiographer of the AME
Church, many saw this as a move to marginalize Turner and to keep him quiet.

Though marginalized, Turner continued to work. His fortunes changed
when the AME Church begrudgingly assigned him to cover a district that needed experienced leadership after the death of its bishop. During his brief tenure,
Turner demonstrated the leadership qualities that endeared him to so many and
Turner did not tone down his fiery rhetoric completely; his lectures focused
more on acceptable topics such as "Science, the Need of the Negro Race." In the
lecture, he would lament the lack of African Americans in the sciences and challenge young people to take up studying science.

In 1913, as African Americans celebrated the fiftieth anniversary of the
Emancipation Proclamation, the AME Church asked him to offer a reflection on
the historical event. While this seemed to be another opportunity for Turner to
criticize the country for not living up to the ideals and principals after the Eman-

cipation, Turner offered an eloquent, moving reflection of the time. Published in the January 1913 edition of the *AME Journal*, Turner's "Reminiscences of the Proclamation of Emancipation," reminded many not only of his legacy and his importance to the AME Church, but also it introduced Turner to a new audience—one that would have only known Turner as pessimistic prophet.

Turner began the essay with fond memories of his introduction to the AME Church. He also wrote about his examination and trial sermon, and how after he withstood some "preacher hazing," Bishop Payne stood up and declared him fit for the ministry. Next, he shared how he and his wife would survive on between "ten and twenty five cents a week" and how he would supplement his income with the "occasional lecture" on physiology.

Turner then reminded his readers that the war was in full blast when he arrived in Washington, D.C. to serve as pastor of Israel Church. He also reminded his readers that also at this time the "rebel army" had the odds of victory in their favor. As pressure began to mount for the enlistment of African Americans, Turner reminded his readers that Israel Church played an important role in recruiting African Americans for the war.

After this, Turner then turned his attention to the day President Lincoln issued the Emancipation. Turner wrote, "The newspapers of the country were prolific and unsparing in their laudations of Mr. Lincoln. Every orator after reviewing in their richest eloquence, concluded their speeches and orations by saying, 'God save Abraham Lincoln,' or 'God bless our President'" ("Reminiscences" 213). After noting the mass meeting that many held throughout the country, Turner concluded, "I may witness such a time again in heaven, but not in the flesh" (213).

At Israel Church, Turner wrote that the "church and its yard were crowded with people." When the people heard the proclamation read aloud Turner wrote, "Every kind of demonstration and gesticulation was going on."

> Men squealed women fainted, dogs barked, white and colored people shook hands, songs were sung . . . every face had a smile, and even the dumb animals seemed to realize that some extraordinary event had taken place. . . . Rumor said that in several instances the very thought of being set at liberty and having no more auction blocks, no more separation of parents and children, no more horrors of slavery, was so elative and heart gladdening that scores of colored people literally fell dead with joy. (214)

Hyperbole aside, Turner's reminiscence of the Emancipation spoke to what he truly longed for in America for African Americans—a chance to be free.

After battling back from a stroke fifteen years earlier, Turner finally succumbed to the effects of another stoke on May 8, 1915 in Windsor, Ontario, Canada while on church business. An estimated twenty-five thousand people viewed the body of Turner when it arrived back in Atlanta. Many religious leaders held services in remembrance of Turner and his legacy. In celebrating the life of Turner after his death, *AME Review* editor Reverdy Ransom remarked that Turner was a "remarkable man, whose like does not appear more than once in a century, the like of whom we shall not see again" (45). Further Ransom wrote:

> Bishop Turner was a staunch defender of his race. His scathing denunciations of lynching and mob violence, his severe arraignments of the courts for unjust decisions and his oppositions to all forms of Jim Crow legislation made him one of the foremost defenders of his race. He stood for the manhood and equality of his race and sought to arouse and stimulate this sentiment among his people. His flaming wrath against traitors, trimmers, sycophants, and cowards among his people revealed the intensity of the fire of his earnestness. (46)

Other contemporaries praised Turner as well. Bishop Evans Tyree in a eulogy of him remarked, "Bishop Turner was a powerful man. He loved his race, his church, and his God from the depths of his soul" while R.R. Wright, Jr., then editor of the *Christian Recorder,* simply wrote, "Henry McNeal Turner was the most remarkable Negro of this generation." Henry Lincoln Johnson, columnist of the newspaper, *The Atlanta Independent* wrote:

> The travail of his people always appealed to Bishop Turner and the lamentations of the negro always found in him an abundant sympathizer and a most distinguish advocate. On the lecture platform, in the public forum, in magazines, in newspapers, indeed everywhere Bishop Turner has brought to bear all of his great learning, research, heart, and soul for the advancement and edification of the Negro the world over. ("Bishop Turner Dead" 1)

W.E.B. Dubois, who would go through a prophetic trajectory similar to Turner, wrote

> [Turner] was a man of tremendous force and indomitable courage. As army chaplain, pastor and bishop, he has always been a man of strength. . . . In a sense, Turner was the last of his clan: mighty men, physically and mentally, men who started at the bottom and hammered their way to the top by sheer brute strength; they were the spiritual progeny of ancient African chieftains and they built the African church in America. (Quoted in Redkey, *Respect* vii-ix)

However, while many remembered him as a dynamic church leader who built the AME Church in the South and while others remembered him for his work in politics, everyone remembered Turner and claimed him as prophet.

Turner's Prophetic Persona

As I have attempted to demonstrate, Henry McNeal Turner's prophetic persona shifted throughout his career. After the Civil War, Turner returned to Georgia and served in the Freedmen's Bureau. Like most blacks at the time, Turner believed the Civil War served two purposes—first, to free the slaves and second, as divine retribution for the sin of slavery. Turner saw the war and its outcome as a monumental shift in the policy of America and believed that all Americans should celebrate emancipation.

Therefore, when asked to keynote the Emancipation Day celebration, Turner adopted a *covenantal/universal prophetic persona*. In other words, Turner saw himself as a prophet to all people, both blacks and whites, and he also saw himself as the conduit that could bring people together under a common cause. Turner saw emancipation as a new day or a new era for both blacks and whites to work together and help America to become the place where anyone could come and find freedom and justice.

In his "Emancipation Day" speech, Turner grounded himself in the sacred identity of America. He argued that America was divinely inspired to "proclaim liberty throughout the land" because it was the "great stone" spoken about in the biblical book of Daniel. It was this argument that helped Turner offer a prophetic reinterpretation of slavery and the war as part of God's providential plan. While slavery was never in harmony with God's laws, Turner argued that God did allow slavery for the civilization of Africans. However, whites failed to adequately civilize and teach the Africans so judgment had to come by way of the Civil War to free blacks. Once freed, blacks could take their place in America's covenantal blessings that were not available to them before.

Turner's hope arose from his belief in America's divine mission. This mission, suppressed during the days of slavery, found a new life after emancipation, and Turner argued that America could live up to its promise of equality. It was within this divine mission that both blacks and whites could work together, and Turner challenged both parties to do so.

It was also this belief that inspired Turner to do his work in Georgia. However, after helping to build the AME Church in Georgia and involving himself in politics, Turner's belief in the American covenant was shaken to its core when he found himself and other black representatives expelled from the Legislature on account of the white representatives' belief in black inferiority. To answer this rejection, Turner, in his 1868 "Eligibility" speech, adopted a prophetic persona that shifted from a *covenantal prophet* to a *representative prophet* who represented the interest of African Americans.

A major change in Turner's rhetoric by 1868 was that Turner no longer grounded himself in the sacredness of the American creed. Though in his "Eligibility" speech he did draw upon the sacredness of the Constitution for political purposes in defining his manhood, from this speech to the end of his career, Turner also grounded himself in the sacredness and sacred character of God. Throughout his career, Turner would expand his conception and interpretation of God to demonstrate that God worked in the lives of the people Turner claimed to represent.

The other noticeable change in Turner's prophetic rhetoric was his conception of encouragement and hope. In his "Emancipation Day" speech, Turner saw the day where both blacks and whites would come together to make the South and America a better place for all. Turner saw blacks working hard and demonstrating their worth to whites, and he saw whites respecting blacks and receiving them into the larger society. The hope promoted in the speech was one of general unity where Turner acted as prophet of both communities.

In his "Eligibility" speech, Turner's hope was in God seeing the injustice of the expulsion and that God would act on behalf of the oppressed African Americans. Turner's hope was that God would act because his opponents had already acted and their action was not only opposed to the American covenant, but also to God's will. Therefore, Turner's hope is for God to act within the covenant that God has with all creation. It was that hope that African Americans could hold onto.

However, by the time of his 1893 "Negro Convention" speech, his prophetic persona again shifted. While he still operated as a *representative prophet* on the behalf of African Americans, Turner became more of a *pragmatic prophet* as he focused more on a plan of action than on calling his audience to celebrate or aim for some covenant. Frustrated by society's dealings with African Americans and annoyed by African American responses to unjust treatment, Turner argued that there was no "manhood" future for blacks in America. While Turner believed that American society would never give equal rights to African Americans, his radically egalitarian commitments to equal rights and inclusion did not wane. In short, Turner believed and supported the principles of America, but argued that African Americans would never have the chance to participate in those principles while in America.

It was Turner's belief that America's unwillingness to live up to the covenant as it related to African Americans, and not the covenant itself, posed a problem. However, since Turner no longer felt a call to be a prophet for America, there was no reason for him to call America to live up to or come back to its covenant. For Turner, America was in an apostate condition that only God could cure. Therefore, in the meantime, African Americans should do all in their power to "seek other quarters."

Finally, in his 1895 "American Negro and his Fatherland" speech Turner's prophetic persona shifted from a pragmatic prophetic to a *pessimistic prophetic* grounded in the lament tradition of prophecy. At this time in his life, Turner had no confidence in American institutions or that the American people would live up to the promises in their sacred documents. While he still argued that emigration was the only way for African Americans to retain their "manhood" status, he also believed that African Americans would never emigrate to Africa. Turner's position limited his rhetorical options, but by adopting a pessimistic prophetic voice Turner found space for his oratory, which reflected itself within the lament tradition of prophecy.

Turner's pessimism continued throughout the rest of his life. As Turner's pessimism grew, he also became bitter and more forceful in his attacks against society and other African Americans who found hope in anti-emigration policies such as integration and accommodation. However, it was within the lament tradition that Turner could still find relevance as an orator by not only offering critiques of society but also offering critiques of black leadership.

By this time, Turner's representative persona shifted from African Americans in general to primarily *Southern blacks*—the ones who faced most of the oppression and the ones more open to emigration. Turner's constant call for emigration would have sounded very hopeful to many people of the South who had nothing to lose, but also just as hopeful were the constant reminders of injustice that affected Southern blacks, because through Turner's oratory, Southern blacks felt heard as well.

To contemporary eyes and ears, a reading of Turner's rhetoric sounds archaic. In many instances, he is mean, crude, cruel, bombastic, and obnoxious. He is at times dogmatic and unwavering in his positions and opinions. However, I suggest that this is not a reason to dismiss Turner; indeed, I suggest that this is the very reason why contemporary audiences should hear Turner's voice. It is out of this bombastic language that Turner professes his love for all people and his desire for America, by way of inclusion in the covenant, or African Americans, by way of emigration, to do the right thing. The very fact that Turner chose to stay in America and continued to live in the South when he could have gone to Africa as a bishop and lived a more comfortable life or moved up North and had a better existence, attested to his prophetic spirit not to give up on himself nor the people he represented.

Another reason to study his rhetoric is that Turner anticipated many of the social movements in African American culture during the twentieth century. W.E.B. DuBois' idea of "cultural nationalism," Marcus Garvey's "Back to Africa Movement," the modern day Civil Rights movement, the Black Power movement, James Cone's Black Theology of Liberation, and even some elements of nationalist rap found in the current hip hop culture, owe a debt to Turner's work and progressive insights.

Moreover, Turner offered a *third way* in African American rhetorical discourse in the late nineteenth and early twentieth centuries. Many historians and rhetoric scholars have called this period of African American history the Washington and DuBois era. Many maintained that African Americans wanted either accommodation or integration. However, Turner rejected both positions and offered emigration as a possible solution to the problems African Americans faced. While the majority of blacks did not accept emigration as a solution, many did. It was through Turner's prophetic pessimism and bearing witness to the ills faced by many African Americans during this time that gave many African Americans a sense of pride and the necessary courage to face whatever came their way.

It is my hope that by examining Turner by weaving both text and context together for analysis, this work will become a springboard for further understanding and study on one of the most important figures in American public address in the nineteenth century.

Notes

1. When news circulated about Turner's comments, many charged him with inciting a race war. Turner responded to his critics in the *Voice of Mission* (May, 1897).

Bibliography

"Affairs in South Carolina." *New York Times*, 5 May 1867.

Anderson, Robert. *The Life of Robert Anderson.* Macon, GA, 1892.

Angell, Stephen W. *Bishop Henry McNeal Turner and African-American Religion in the South.* Knoxville: University of Tennessee Press, 1992.

————. "Black Methodist Preachers in the South Carolina Upcountry, 1840-1866: Isaac (Counts) Cook, James Porter, and Henry McNeal Turner." In *Ain't Gonna Lay My 'Ligion Down: African American Religion in the South,* edited by Alonzo Johnson and Paul Jersild, 87-109. Columbia, SC: University of South Carolina Press, 1996.

Batten, J. Minton. "Henry McNeal Turner, Negro Bishop Extraordinary." *Church History* 8 (1938): 231-146

Bercovitch, Sacvan. *The American Jeremiad.* Madison: University of Wisconsin Press, 1978.

"Bishop Turner's Wail." *Cleveland Gazette,* 18 July 1896.

Bitzer, Lloyd. "The Rhetorical Situation." In *Contemporary Rhetorical Theory: A Reader,* edited by John Louis Lucaites Celeste Michelle Condit, and Sally Caudill, 217-225. New York: The Guilford Press, 1999.

Carter, Dan. "The Anatomy of Fear: The Christmas Day Insurrection Scare of 1865." *Journal of Southern History* 42.3 (1976): 345-364.

Cimprich, John. "The Beginning of the Black Suffrage Movement in Tennessee, 1864-65." *Journal of Negro History* 65.3 (1980): 185-195.

"Colored Chaplain: Rev. H.M. Turner." *New York Times,* 14 Nov. 1863.

"The Colored Convention in Augusta." *Milledgeville Southern Recorder*, 30 Jan. 1866.

Condit, Celeste Michelle and John Louis Lucaites. *Crafting Equality: America's Anglo-African Word.* Chicago: University of Chicago Press, 1993.

Culp, D.W., ed. *Twentieth Century Negro Literature.* Naperville, IL: J.L. Nichols and Co., 1902.

Dantley, Michael. "Purpose Driven Leadership: The Spiritual Imperative to Guiding Schools Beyond High-Stakes Testing and Minimum Proficiency." *Education and Urban Society* 35.3 (2003): 273-91.

Darsey, James. *The Prophetic Tradition and Radical Rhetoric in America.* New York: New York University Press, 1997.

Dittmer, John. "The Education of Henry McNeal Turner." in *Black Leaders of the Nineteenth Century*, edited by Leon Litwack and August Meier, 253-274. Chicago: University of Illinois Press, 1991

Douglass, Frederick. *Lessons of the Hour.* Washington, D.C.: Thomas and Evans, 1894.

Foucault, Michel. *Fearless Speech.* Los Angeles, California: Semiotext(e), 2001.

Foster, Gaines M. *Ghosts of the Confederacy: Defeat, The Lost Cause, and the Emergence of the New South 1865 to 1913.* New York: Oxford University Press, 1987.

Fredrickson, George M. *The Black Image in the White Mind: The Debate of Afro-American Character and Destiny 1817-1914.* New York: Harper and Row, 1971.

"Freedmen's Convention." *Loyal Georgian,* 20 Jan. 1866.

"From Rev. H.M. Turner." *Christian Recorder,* 17 Aug. 1867.

Graffy, Adrian. *Prophet Confronts His People: The Disputation Speech in the Prophets.* Vol. 104, *Analecta Biblica.* Loyola Pub., 1984.

Gravely, William B. "The Dialectic of Double-Consciousness in Black American Freedom Celebrations, 1808-1863." *Journal of Negro History* 67.4 (1982): 302-317.

Greenberg, Kenneth S. *Masters and Statesmen: The Political Culture of American Slavery.* Baltimore: Johns Hopkins University Press, 1985.

Hanson, Paul D. "The Origin and Nature of Prophetic Political Engagement in Ancient Israel." In *Let Justice Roll: Prophetic Challenges in Religion, Politics, and Society,* edited by Neal Riemer, 1-22. Lanham, MD: Rowman and Littlefield Publishers, 1996.

Haley, James T. *Afro-American Encyclopedia.* Nashville: Haley and Florida, 1895.

Herndon, Jane W. "Henry McNeal Turner: Exponent of American Negritude." M.A. thesis, Georgia State College, 1967.

Heschel, Abraham J. *The Prophets.* New York: Harper and Row, 1955.

Hinton, Thomas H.C. "From Washington." *Christian Recorder,* 4 July 1863.

———. "Washington Correspondence." *Christian Recorder,* 8 Aug. 1863.

———. "Washington Correspondence." *Christian Recorder,* 3 Oct. 1863.

Holmes, Barbara A. "For Such a Time as This: Lament as a Herald of Joy." Princeton Youth Lectures, Seattle, WA, January 2006.

Howard-Pitney, David. *The Afro-American Jeremiad: Appeal for Justice in America.* Philadelphia: Temple University Press, 1990.

Jenkins, William Sumner. *Pro-Slavery Thought in the Old South.* Chapel Hill: University of North Carolina Press, 1935.

Johnson, Andre E. ed. *An African American Pastor Before and During the American Civil War: The Literary Archive of Henry McNeal Turner,* vol. 1. New York: Edwin Mellen Press, 2010.

———. *An African American Pastor Before and During the American Civil War: The Literary Archive of Henry McNeal Turner,* vol. 2. New York: Edwin Mellen Press

———. *The Prophetic Oratory of Henry McNeal Turner.* Ph.D. diss., University of Memphis, 2008.

———. "The Prophetic Persona of James Cone and the Rhetorical Theology of Black Theology." *Black Theology Journal* 8.3 (2010): 266-285.

———. "Will We Have Ears to Hear: the African American Prophetic Tradition in the Age of Obama." *African American Pulpit* (Spring 2010): 10-14.

Johnson, Henry Lincoln. "Bishop Turner Dead." *Atlanta Independent,* 15 May 1915.

Kent, Robert. F. "Letter from Augusta." *Christian Recorder,* 27 Jan. 1866.

Lampe, George. *Frederick Douglass: Freedom's Voice 1818-1845.* East Lansing, MI: Michigan State University Press, 1998.

Lawrence, Windy. "A Crisis in Civil Rights Leadership: The Prophetic Persona in Lyndon B. Johnson's Howard University Address." *Texas Speech Communication Journal* 31 (2007): 35-43

Leeman, Richard W. "Speaking as Jeremiah: Henry McNeal Turner's I Claim the Rights of a Man." *Howard Journal of Communications* 17 (2006): 223-243.

Leff, Michael. "Textual Criticism: The Legacy of G.P. Mohrmann." *Quarterly Journal of Speech* 72 (1986): 377-389.

Logan, Shirley Wilson. *Sites of Rhetorical Education in Nineteenth-Century Black America.* Carbondale: Southern Illinois University Press, 2008.

Logue, Cal. "Rhetorical Ridicule of Reconstruction Blacks." *Quarterly Journal of Speech* 62 4 (1976): 400-409

Martin, Elmer. "The Life of Henry McNeal Turner, 1834 to 1870." M.A. thesis, Florida State University, 1975.

McClure, Kevin R. "Frederick Douglass' Use of Comparison in His Fourth of July Oration: A Textual Criticism." *Western Journal of Communication* 64 (Fall 2000): 425-445.

McKerrow, Raymie E. "Critical Rhetoric: Theory and Praxis." *Communication Monographs* 56 (June 1989): 91-111.

McLaren, Peter L and Michael Dantley. "Leadership and a Critical Pedagogy of Race: Cornel West, Stuart Hall, and the Prophetic Tradition." *Journal of Negro Education* 59.1 (1990): 29-44.

Mixon, Gregory. "Henry McNeal Turner versus the Tuskegee Machine: Black Leadership in the Nineteenth Century." *Journal of Negro History* 7.4 (1994): 363-380.

Moses, Wilson Jeremiah. *Black Messiahs and Uncle Toms: Social and Literary Manipulations of a Religious Myth.* University Park: The Pennsylvania State University Press, 1982.

"Negroes Get Guns." *New York Times*, 17 March 1897.

Nieman, Donald G. *Promises to Keep: African-Americans and the Constitutional Order, 1776 to the Present.* New York: Oxford University Press, 1991.

"The Political Situation in South Carolina—Speeches by Governor Orr and Others." *Baltimore Sun*, 30 Apr. 1867.

122   Bibliography

Ponton, Mungo M. Life and Times of Henry McNeal Turner. New York: Negro Universities Press, 1970.

Ransom, Reverdy C. "Bishop Henry McNeal Turner." *The Henry McNeal Turner Collection,* box 1, folder 2. Manuscript Division, Moorland-Spingarn Research Center, Howard University.

Redkey, Edwin. *Black Exodus: Black Nationalist and Back to Africa Movements, 1890-1910.* New Haven: Yale University Press, 1969.

———. "Henry McNeal Turner: Black Chaplain in the Union Army." In *Black Soldiers in Blue: African American Troops in the Civil War Era,* edited by John David Smith, 336-60. Chapel Hill: UNC Press, 2004.

———. *Respect Black: The Writings and Speeches of Henry McNeal Turner.* New York: Arno Press, 1971.

Reid, Ronald F. "Apocalypticism and Typology: Rhetorical Dimensions of a Symbolic Reality." *The Quarterly Journal of Speech* 69 (1983): 229-248.

"Rev. H.M. Turner." *Harper's Weekly,* 13 Dec. 1863, 8.

Sanger, Kerran L. "Slave Resistance and Rhetorical Self-Definition: Spiritual as a Strategy." *Western Journal of Communication* 59 (1995): 177-192.

Saunders, M.G. "Highly Interesting from Georgia." *Christian Recorder,* 21 July 1866.

Simmons, William J. *Men of Mark: Eminent, Progressive and Rising.* Cleveland: Geo. M. Rewell and Co., 1887.

Smith, H. Sheldon. *In His Image, But . . . : Racism in Southern Religion, 1790-1910.* Durham, NC: Duke University Press, 1972.

Tanner, Benjamin. *An Apology for African Methodism.* Baltimore, 1867.

———. "Bishop Turner on the Advisory Committee." *Christian Recorder,* 4 Jan. 1883.

———. "Bishop Turner's Reply." *Christian Recorder,* 2 Feb. 1883.

Terrill, Robert E. *Malcolm X: Inventing Radical Judgment.* East Lansing, MI: Michigan State University Press, 2004.

———. "Symbolic Emancipation in the Rhetoric of Malcolm X." Ph.D. diss., Northwestern University, 1996.

Turner, Henry McNeal. *African Letters.* Nashville: AME Publishing House, 1893.

———. "The American Negro and the Fatherland." In *Africa and the American Negro: Addresses and Proceedings of the Congress on Africa,* edited by J.W.E. Bowen, 195-198. Atlanta: Franklin Printing and Publishing Company, 1896.

———. "Bishop Turner Tells." *Indianapolis Freedman,* 13 Jan. 1894 .

———. *Celebration of the First Anniversary of Freedom.* Augusta, GA: G.U.L. of Georgia, 1866.

———. *Civil Rights: The Outrage of the Supreme Court of the United States upon the Black Man.* Philadelphia: AME Publishing House 1889.

———. "A Colored National Convention." *Voice of Missions,* 1 Aug. 1893.

——. *Emigration of the Colored People of the United States: Is it Expedient? If so Where To?* Philadelphia: AME Publishing House, 1879.

——. "From Chaplain Turner." *Christian Recorder,* 25 June 1864.

——. "Home of the Blacks: Liberia the Place for the Negro to Nationalize Himself." *Voice of Missions*, March 1895.

——. "Is the Negro a Fool?" *Voice of Missions*, Nov. 1898.

——. "Lazy Preachers a Curse." *Voice of Missions*, Aug. 1899.

——. "Letter to E.M. Stanton." 1 Aug. 1863. National Archives and Records Administration: Colored Troops Division: RG 94, Washington, D.C.

——. "Letter to E.M. Stanton." 30 June 1864. National Archive and Records Administration: Letters Received, ser. 12, RG 94.

——. "McKinley, The God of Fool Negroes, Re-Elected." *Voice of Missions*, Dec. 1900.

——. "Negro Convention Speech: Emigration or Justice." *Voice of Missions*, 1 Dec. 1893.

——. "The Negro Should Not Enter the Army." *Voice of Missions*, May 1899.

——. *On the Present Duties and Future Destiny of the Negro Race.* Savannah, GA, 1872.

——. "To Colored People." *Atlanta Constitution*, 13 Jan. 1895.

——. "A Very Important Letter." *Christian Recorder*, 9 July 1864.

Tyree, Evans. "Bishop Tyree Delivers Eulogy." *The Henry McNeal Turner Collection,* box 1, folder 2. Manuscript Division, Moorland-Spingarn Research Center, Howard University.

Walzer, Michael. "Prophecy and Social Criticism." In *Let Justice Roll: Prophetic Challenges in Religion, Politics, and Society,* edited by Neal Riemer, 23-37. Lanham, MD: Rowman and Littlefield Publishers, 1996.

Washington, Booker T. "Speech at the Cotton States and International Exposition Commonly called the Atlanta Compromise." Atlanta, 1895.

West, Cornel. *Prophetic Fragments: Illuminations of the Crisis in American Religion and Culture.* Grand Rapids, MI: Wm. B. Eerdmans Publishing Company, 1988.

——. "The Prophetic Tradition in Afro America." In *Let Justice Roll: Prophetic Challenges in Religion, Politics, and Society,* edited by Neal Riemer, 89-100. Lanham, MD: Rowman and Littlefield Publishing, 1996.

W.H.M. "Washington Correspondence." *Christian Recorder*, 4 Apr. 1863.

Wilson, Kirt H. *The Reconstruction Desegregation Debate: The Politics of Equality and the Rhetoric of Place, 1870-1875.* East Lansing, MI: Michigan State University Press, 2002.

Wright, R. R. Bishop. "H.M.Turner." *The Henry McNeal Turner Collection,* box 1, folder 2. Manuscript Division, Moorland-Spingarn Research Center, HowardUniversity.

Index